Married to King Saul

Married to King Saul

A Woman's Quest to Understand Her Abusive Husband

NATHALIE ELVIRE GAILLOT

RESOURCE *Publications* · Eugene, Oregon

MARRIED TO KING SAUL
A Woman's Quest to Understand Her Abusive Husband

Resource Publications
An Imprint of Wipf and Stock Publishers
199 W. 8th Ave., Suite 3
Eugene, OR 97401

www.wipfandstock.com

PAPERBACK ISBN: 978-1-6667-1150-9
HARDCOVER ISBN: 978-1-6667-1151-6
EBOOK ISBN: 978-1-6667-1152-3

09/22/21

Copyeditor: Emily Tope
Reviewer: Diana Moen

Author's Note:
I would like to state that this memoir is my best recollection of events that happened in my life and aims to provide help for those who fall victim to domestic violence. It is written from my perspective and is not meant to inflict harm on any person based on character representation.

Unless otherwise noted, all Scripture citations are from the King James Version.

This book is for all the women who have lived through the pain of domestic violence. I hope my story will encourage you and help you in your healing journey.

This book is for my children, so they understand that as I loved their father, I loved them too. I am very thankful for the people that you have become; you have endured a lot and are amazing. I love you so much.

This book is for all the young people who bear the scars of their parents' abusive relationship and still wear the shoes of the powerless children they once were. I want you to know that you do not have to repeat the past, that God loves you, and that you can have a glorious future. May you know that you were loved from the beginning and that God watches over you, always.

Contents

Acknowledgments

I AM SO GRATEFUL for the friends, family members, and people in pastoral authority who have offered me support through the years—with or without being aware of my circumstances—be it with their wise counsel, their friendship, or their kindness. When you are navigating the dangerous waters of domestic abuse, a smile can be just the touch of God that you need at the moment. To those who have taken the time to review this memoir and give me feedback, I am very thankful. I would like to thank in particular my friend Diana Moen. Last, but certainly not least, I am most thankful and indebted to God, who has sustained me and rescued me time and time again, and kept me alive, safe, and full of faith for what the future holds.

Abbreviations

BC	before Christ
Cor	Corinthians
CT	Computed Tomography
Eccl	Ecclesiastes
Eph	Ephesians
Ezek	Ezekiel
Gal	Galatians
HCP	High Conflict Personality
Hos	Hosea
Jas	James
Matt	Matthew
NKJV	New King James Version
Pet	Peter
Prov	Proverbs
Rom	Romans
Sam	Samuel

Introduction

"What has been will be again, what has been done will be done again; there is nothing new under the sun."

—Eccl 1:9

Life has a way of taking you places you didn't plan on going, like a rip current sweeps you from the shallows into the depths of the ocean. It is only there that you learn to swim or resign yourself to drowning. In these moments, life can lead you to be who you didn't want to become, repeating others' mistakes, your parents' failures, and the history of human misbehaviors. Perhaps the biggest life lesson is to learn to make peace with your past in order to strive to do better.

I, for one, never expected to be caught in an abusive relationship and find myself at a loss for directions, especially as a Christian. Both God and humans teach us that there is a right and a wrong. Within this dichotomy, domestic abuse falls on the "wrong" end of the spectrum. It seems logical to stand up against violence and protect the weak: women, children, oneself. But if, like me, you *are* that person trapped in a destructive relationship, you lose sight of your moral compass as you focus on staying afloat in deep and dangerous waters. I have learned it is easier to figure out someone else's circumstances—to judge and develop empirical opinions about what people should do in certain situations—than our own. The truth is, we don't have the answers until we experience those situations and discover that behind what appears to be a clear-cut choice of right or wrong lies the complexity of our subjectivity. Each of us possesses layers of thoughts, emotions, needs, and dreams that are unique to the self; when something bad happens to us, we are the only ones who can take the first steps to improve our situation. And yet, as contradictory as this sounds, we also need each other to find clarity. God placed us on this earth to help ourselves and one another.

Proverbs 11:14 reads, "Where no counsel is, the people fall: but in the multitude of counsellors there is safety." When you are, or have been, in an abusive relationship, it is important to turn to people who have personally experienced abuse or worked with women and men in abusive situations. It is likewise important to read books about psychology and self-help to uncover the cycle of abuse. Both resources help you understand what goes on in the human mind and how patterns of narcissistic behavior and co-dependent relationships form. They also offer advice for making escape plans and creating steps for practical change, be it the resolution of the abusive behaviors, or the end of the relationship. The most likely scenarios that will end abuse in a marriage are repentance and healing, divorce, or, in extreme cases, homicide.

As is the case with most difficult choices, whether you choose to stay and fight for a marriage in which you are walking on eggshells or are in more imminent danger, or to leave, it is important that you make the choice yourself, with knowledge, faith, and no regrets. This means that you can only make choices at the time you are in, with the resources and the information you have. Nowhere in Scripture is abuse condoned by God. As believers, we seek God's guidance in all things, and for that reason the best answers are those found in his Word. Only he can give full meaning to our lives and reveal the ultimate direction he has for us.

As we walk along our own paths in Christ, sharing personal stories helps us understand that we are not alone, even if we face unique circumstances. Stories provide an objective lens, a broader understanding, which in turn helps us consider others' experiences, make decisions, and find healing. To understand God's will for my life and find direction, I like to turn to the stories narrated in the Bible to see where I can identify with the characters, because I believe that everything that can happen to me in this lifetime has happened to others before me and is covered in the Word of God.

For a long time, I searched the Bible for a story that would mirror my own, to help me make sense of what was happening in my life as a devoted Christian wife and give me a reason to keep my faith that God would heal my abusive husband. I looked in Scripture to give myself grounds to ask God for his miraculous intervention so that I would have the faith that pleases him and would cause him to move mountains. I held God at his Word to find that which was broken and heal that which was sick. I also wanted God to make of my broken marriage a fairy tale ending where we lived happily ever after.

God has already performed many miracles in my life. I know him to be Jehovah Rapha, healer; Jehovah Jireh, provider; and Jehovah Nissi, protector. It took some time to find where my story was written in the Word of

God, but be assured it is there, because there is nothing that has not already been considered by God, and nothing that he does not have answers for, for otherwise he would not be God. We can look, ponder, ask, seek, and ultimately find. God answers prayers, he answers questions, and he instructs us.

I found understanding in the book of First Samuel, with a replica of my broken marriage hidden in the relationship between David and King Saul. It took a while to see it because it is not about a marriage or even a romantic bond; yet all the elements of love, loyalty, jealousy, abuse, and the quest for God's favor and blessings are present.

The Old Testament tells the story of a man named Saul, chosen by God to be the first king of Israel around 1050 BC. Saul was an extraordinary man: he was strong and charismatic, but also impetuous, rebellious, and mad; he was filled with the Spirit of God, but also tormented by an evil spirit. I find in Saul an archetype of my abusive husband, and in the story of King Saul answers to questions I have struggled with for years: What is wrong with my husband? Why does he not change? Why does God not remold him when I pray for him so fervently?

My story is that of a woman who loves her husband, but also fears him. It tells of her hopes, her fights, her fears, and her relentless love for a man whom many will find unlovable, but who is a broken soul no less in need of a savior than anyone else. We serve a God who is love incarnate, who ransomed his own son in order to save all humankind through the offer of redemption. We are all sinners in need of Christ's redemption—including those with abusive personalities.

To share the story of my abusive marriage, I have chosen to portray fictional characters, so as to preserve the anonymity of people in my life, and to give myself some distance from the memories of difficult psychological experiences. To that end, the names of the characters are fictitious as well. As I share my story, I will also recount in parallel the story of King Saul from the Bible, in my own voice, and focus on the specific characteristics that Saul exhibits—characteristics that are shared by abusive personalities, including the character in my story. As the two stories progress in parallel, each chapter focuses on one specific trait that is not in and of itself a sign of an abusive personality, but which may constitute a red flag when several other traits are present together. Paying attention to those signs early in a relationship may help you confront issues sooner rather than later.

My hope is to help you look to Scripture to seek the answers that you are waiting for as you live your story, as you walk this life holding on to your relationship with Jesus. The Word of God as quoted at the beginning of this introduction promises that the personal struggles that we go through are common stories that tie us together. If you cannot relate directly to this story, may the information you gain by reading it help you view abusive individuals with compassion, and abused women with understanding, so you may perhaps help someone else to move forward.

If you are in an abusive situation, or want to help someone else, I hope that you will use common sense with your conversations with friends, family, and others who have walked in your shoes before you; and most importantly, when you find where your story is narrated in the Word of God, may you rest assured that he will walk with you through the good, the bad, and the miraculous.

Prologue

"You should write a book about me."

Loammi was standing by his equipment, cleaning every inch of his recorder, front to back, wiping each outlet with the expert precision of a practiced musician, and pulling through the cords with the roughness of a "manly" man.

"I'm serious, babe. You should write a book about me. People wouldn't believe the life I've had; they just wouldn't believe it! Imagine that—my mama didn't want me when I was born. I was just a baby, there's nothing wrong I could have done, and she rejected me! And you know how much that hurts to know your own mama didn't even want you? It's like I was set up for failure from the beginning. And my daddy, he didn't even think I was his son; he even said so himself. Listen to this, babe. One day, I was just about a teenager, right? Well, my daddy took me out with my uncle, and they were all drinking, then my dad said to me: 'You should ask your mama about Sam.' I had no idea what he was talking about, but when I asked my uncle, he told me my dad thought this Sam guy was someone my mom was involved with and that I wasn't even his child but that Sam's kid! Do you know how much that hurts to have your own dad not even believe that you're his son? I look just like him and yet it's like he had that doubt in his mind all his life that I wasn't even his. The fool!

"But . . . I forgave them, thanks be to God; I've forgiven both him and my mom. I don't hate them for that; I'm not holding nothing against them. I love them. I've had the worst life, but you know, it was beautiful too! I had the ugly and the beautiful, the worst and the best. My daddy was a pimp; my granddaddy was a preacher. It's like God and the Devil put a bet on me and were fighting for my soul. I was raised with the good and the bad. Back then we had nothing, but we'd always come together; there was always joy and laughter. It was so fun back then to be a kid; life was so simple! The community, it was beautiful; people looked out for each other—not like how it is today, with everyone shooting each other. The doors were always open

1

at my aunt's house. It didn't matter who you were; if you had nothing to eat you could come in and eat and find a moment of joy and rest from your tribulations . . . Ah, it was so beautiful!"

Loammi sighed. With dusk setting in, it was hard to tell if a tear was forming in the corner of his eye, or simply the contrast between the sudden darkness and the light of his retina made it sparkle. Marine was always fascinated when listening to him, though it did occur to her to turn the lights on. But she did not want to interrupt him, so she kept on listening in the dark.

"And yet it was crazy, too, you know. I had the ugly and the beautiful! The best and the worst. Sometimes I wonder if we already existed before we were created on this earth, and I just asked God to give me the worst, you know, like I thought I could handle it, and I just asked him to give me the worst. Or else it is God who has a sick sense of humor, like he did with Job? Sometimes I wonder: maybe this life we live is just a bet between God and the Devil? After all, isn't there something sick about allowing the Devil to come and say 'oh, here, let me take everything this man has and loves,' just to test and see if you're going to praise God? I mean, it doesn't make sense, but part of me wonders sometimes if God isn't just toying with us, as if there is a pact between him and the Devil, and wouldn't that just be sick?

"But babe, I know God is real. No one has gone through all I've gone through and hasn't lost his mind. God has been the only one I've been able to rely on, and he's always been there for me! But the Devil has been there too. I've told you before, but let me tell you again, because it's important that you really understand me, baby. When I was a kid, I saw the Devil face to face, through the kitchen window. I was about five years old and my grandma was sitting in another room, probably praising God. And the Devil appeared to me; I saw him through the window! I was so scared, I wanted to scream for my grandma, but the sounds barely came out of my mouth. And I swear, since then, he's been out there all my life trying to make sure that I don't succeed. He's always been trying to take away everything I have, and everything I love . . . "

Loammi's shadow blocked the last glimmer of light left coming through the window. He had interrupted his cleaning and since he had detached the wires from his keyboards and recorder, they were now hanging loose.

Marine got up and turned the light on. She stopped listening to him when he started talking about the Devil. Why did he always have to go there? Everyone knows the Devil exists, but why pay so much attention to him? Why display such a fascination toward him? It's creepy! Certainly, Loammi was right about the fact that there is a battle for our souls, but God tells us that if we just resist the enemy rather than marvel at his wit, he will flee. Besides, once she intellectualized his stories, she could see the flaw in his argument: not everything is the Devil's fault. In fact, many times, it's our own fault, and our problems are the simple consequences of poor choices we make in life. How could Loammi not see that? She would have spoken up, but it was hard to have intellectual discussions with Loammi, for he had intense emotions and did not seem to comprehend others' points of view.

Nonetheless, Marine loved listening to him. Not only was he a good storyteller, he *did* have very challenging circumstances in life, and she had learned so much, about God, about music, about life as black men and women in America, and most importantly, about Loammi's heart. In fact, Marine was often amazed, and very proud that he had turned out to be so persistent in his quest to be a man of God, in spite of all that he had gone through. He could have been a drug dealer or a pimp, a gang member or a murderer. But instead, he was a songwriter; he used music to express his pain and channel his love—to do something for God.

After all, his mission was important, and she tried her best to support it. In fact, he was doing more for God than Marine was; after all, writing songs for the down-and-out giving credit to God was a way of working directly for God. Marine, meanwhile, was pursuing a secular degree and did nothing directly for Jesus. Someday soon, Loammi would accomplish a great goal. She was counting on it.

"You should write a book about me, babe."

"I will, honey, as soon as I'm done with my dissertation," joked Marine.

1

The Charmer

"For the Scripture saith unto Pharaoh, Even for this same purpose have I raised thee up, that I might shew my power in thee, and that my name might be declared throughout all the earth."

—Rom 9:17

THE STORY OF KING Saul is recorded in the Bible in the book of First Samuel. In 1050 BC, Israel was ruled by prophets called Judges. Though the Judges had been appointed by God to rule directly under his authority, there was no centralized government, and as a result, there was a lack of direct leadership. Samuel, the son of Hannah, had succeeded the prophet Eli and reigned over Israel for nearly twenty years. He was just, righteous, and highly favored by God, who spoke to him directly. But he was getting old, and his sons did not follow the ways of the Lord. Therefore, the leaders of Israel begged him to appoint a king over them. This was an offense toward God, but the Lord told Samuel to heed their demand.

God himself selected the man who would become the very first King of Israel. As if to mark this extraordinary appointment, God picked the most handsome and valiant man of all—a man named Saul.

Although Saul was a Benjamite, which means that he belonged to the smallest tribe of Israel, his social status was high. His father, Kish, was known as "a mighty man of power" (1 Sam 9:2). Saul himself was of exceptional physical build, described as "a choice young man, and a goodly." The Bible *emphasizes that Saul was taller than any of his peers in all of Israel, and there was not in the land a more attractive and admirable young man than he was. Saul's good looks fit the profile of a king: he was strong, he was charismatic, and most importantly, he was appointed by God.*

God led Saul to the prophet Samuel, who anointed him with holy oil and prophesied over him. It says in the Word of God that as Saul walked away from Samuel, "God gave him another heart." Then the Spirit of the Lord came upon him and he prophesied. The transformation that occurred in Saul in the Old Testament brings to mind the transformation that takes place today when a person gives his or her heart to Jesus and becomes a new creature in Christ. As surely as those who have profaned against God are renewed (Ezek 36:26), or those who have been converted to Christ are transformed (2 Cor 5:17), Saul was now marked by God.

Saul was approximately thirty years old when he began his reign, which means that he was in the prime of his life; not too young to lack wisdom, nor too old to lack strength. His power and physical strength certainly contributed to his popularity, but he was also a humble and a righteous man, so the people honored him, recognizing in his character the goodness of God.

The spirit that the Lord had placed in him gave Saul the ability to use wisdom and self-control before his enemies, the sons of Belial. Before Samuel had crowned him king, Saul had already proven that he possessed a righteous character: when Nahash the Ammonite, who controlled the city of Ammon, east of Israel, went into Israeli territory and threatened to take away the right eye of the inhabitants of Jabesh-Gilead in exchange for peace, Saul was angered. It is said that the anger of the Lord, which is a righteous anger, came over him. He planned a surprise attack and defeated the Ammonites, protecting his people before he had even officially been crowned! It was after that victory that Saul was sworn king before God almighty and before the men of Israel by Samuel the prophet. A huge and victorious celebration took place in honor of King Saul!

Afterward, Saul's popularity grew within Israel. He was honored and loved by the people of Israel, who could not have wished for a better king.

God allowed Samuel to reign by Saul's side in order to remind the people, who had asked for a king, to not forget God's commandments. Samuel forewarned the Israelites that as long as they did not forsake the Lord, he would be with them and with their king, Saul. However, if they departed from his commandments, the hand of God would be against them. (1 Sam 8–12)

MARINE WAS AN EXCHANGE student in her late twenties, pursuing a doctoral degree in liberal arts at the university. She came from France. When she mentioned France, most people assumed that she was from Paris, but in fact she came from the outskirts of Lyon, a big city near the French Alps. There, she grew up with two siblings and two parents, in a small house halfway between the city and the countryside. She knew what it was like to walk across town to buy a fresh *demi-baguette* or a *flûte* bread from the *boulangerie* (bakery), to face down stray dogs in the middle of the rural streets that led out of the city center, to wave to the cows on the drive out of her hometown, and to ride a bike all day looking for a friend to hang out with on those quiet Sunday afternoons. She was also familiar with the busier and more polluted city life by being so close to Lyon, the "city of lights."

Marine had lived a rather conventional childhood in France. She was raised in a middle-class household, and she lived in a small house with a yard and the equivalent of a picket fence: a good old-fashioned French *grillage*, made of green wire mesh. Her father was a hard worker who enjoyed a balanced life of intellectual challenges, leisure, and physical activities; her mother took care of the home and cooked two meals every day, while working part-time. The family had enough means to meet their basic needs, take care of bills, and go on an annual summer vacation during the three-to-five weeks that French workers typically take off in the months of July and August. Every year, they would go camping by the Mediterranean Sea or the Atlantic Ocean. Sometimes it was in the mountains: the nearby Alps, the Jura, or the Vosges up north. Objectively speaking, Marine lived well; yet she spent her childhood looking forward to being emancipated and having a life of her own someday. In principle, she loved her family, but her parents fought all the time and her dad was strict. There was often tension at home. She envied her friends who appeared to have what she thought was a "normal" family; she dreamed of having one of those herself when she grew up. In fact, she believed that life truly started for her when she turned eighteen and went to college.

She had learned English and German at school and dreamed of living abroad. Enamored with the foggy weather of London, she would gladly have moved there, if it wasn't for the food she had experienced when she visited England. Nonetheless, the black-and-white photograph of the London bridge that she had personally taken, developed, and framed hung on her bedroom wall as a daily reminder that someday she would go somewhere new. After getting a degree in English literature from the University of Lyon, an opportunity to study in the United States arose and Marine took it.

When she arrived in the United States, Marine was not a Christian. In fact, she did not think much about religion. To her, the freedom of religion modeled by French institutions felt like a system of incarceration.

Historically, her country had been built on the Catholic faith, which to her resembled more a conquest for power and empirical gain than a mission of salvation. In that way, it was similar to the pre-eighteenth-century European wars that determined the national boundaries until the Enlightenment, which freed people from the despotism of religion and led to the French Revolution, which brought further freedom from the nepotism of kings and clergy. Therefore, at the end of the twentieth century, France was a country that called itself Catholic but promoted laicity. It was in that environment that Marine had grown up.

A scholar, she thought of Christians as either goody two shoes who had no intellectual freedom or weak-minded sect-followers who were taken advantage of by self-serving charlatans. She knew for sure that any conversations she had ever had with professing Christians were awkward at best, just like the one she had had just a few days before with an old woman who had approached her while she was waiting for the bus. At that time, Marine had been in America for seven years. She had almost finished her master's degree and had lived through the disillusions of a romance that left her with a three-year-old child and the determination to juggle her studies, work, and motherhood all on her own, all while hoping for some support to come her way. As she was waiting for the bus, keeping to herself and tending to her little boy in a stroller, an elderly woman approached her out of nowhere.

Marine had felt embarrassed when the woman blurted out, after she had reluctantly told the woman her name, "Do you know Jesus Christ, Marine?" Perhaps it was the fact that the old lady looked a little crazy, or else that the name of Jesus was embarrassing to her, but Marine had been concerned about what the people around her must have been thinking. She was a right-minded, intellectual young woman and did not wish to be associated—especially not in front of a crowd of sensible people—with this overzealous Jesus freak. She did reluctantly converse with this woman until the bus pulled up and rescued her from the embarrassing conversation. When she got on the bus, the old woman waived at her and shouted, "I will pray for you, Marine."

Years later, Marine would come to believe that that woman was an angel that God had sent to save her soul. This is how it happened. One day in January, in the upper Midwest, she was walking through a blizzard, tightening the hood of her coat around her head. On the other side of the street stood a tall man also dressed in several layers of winter clothes to keep the biting wind off his flesh. As Marine crossed the street toward him, she saw the big smile on his face. The contrast between the darkness of his skin and the brightness of his smile, as well as flickers of light in his eyes, surprised her. Neither of them could see the other very well, but it felt as if a spark flew up as she passed by. Something very strange happened to Marine at that moment—an unsought thought entered her head: "God, if this man is available, can he be mine?" Marine dismissed this strange thought as surely as if she had let it out of her head altogether; she didn't know *why* she had thought that, nor could she even see the guy clearly! Yet, the man, now behind her, had turned around and called out to her, as if he had had a parallel thought:

"I'm sorry, I normally don't do this, but I felt like something told me to talk to you. My name is Loammi. What is your name?"

That is how it started. After giving him her number, Marine carried on with her day, and when she visited a friend later, she told him: "I think I just met my future husband."

THE ROMANTIC RELATIONSHIP BETWEEN Loammi and Marine developed rapidly. Marine had never met a man like him. He was intense, strong in his principles, somewhat forceful, and unlike her, he knew exactly where and what he stood for; in essence, he was the opposite of her. Raised in the rural suburbs of South Side, Chicago, by his grandmother and his aunt, this aspiring musician dressed like a movie star from the seventies, with ironed shirts and suits that had a wide open collar on the chest and embraced his legs like a snug fit. But what was most shocking to her was that he dared to wear bright colors that made him stand out from other men. That surprised Marine because French fashion is elegant and subtle, and does not scream for attention like Loammi's clothes did. Aside from his attire, Loammi had a different mindset than Marine. It was as if he were free, released from social conventions and etiquette. He knew how to get bargain-priced jewelry and electronics at pawn shops, and he ate unhealthy southern American foods in which taste was disguised with butter and hot sauce. He did not appreciate shrimp, salads, quiche, brie, or wine, and most shockingly, he was not a scholar nor did he know other languages. The one common interest the pair had was playing chess. Loammi always joked that a matchmaker would never have put them together—only God could do something like that!

Though they did not share many interests, the couple had deep conversations. Marine was fascinated by Loammi's ability to tell stories. For someone who did not graduate from high school, Loammi had a way with words, and while he did not have an extensive vocabulary that included words like "inauspicious" and "epistemology," he knew how to pierce a string in your heart with simple locutions and images. That talent was evidenced in the lyrics of the many songs that he had composed.

"Come hear this song, baby; I just wrote it last night! It's called 'If I love you forever.'"

Marine loved to listen to his songs. She could honestly say that just about all of them were her favorites. Loammi wrote about poignant subjects such as the plight of African Americans ostracized in ghettos, the pain of unreciprocated love, and the fight of the inner soul to tell right from wrong. The only songs that she did not like were those that were too appealing to the masses—those that contained sexual innuendos or made him sound arrogant. His style varied from blues to rap songs. One day she had asked him if he was a "rappist."

"You mean, a *rapper*," he had laughed. "Not really. I am not contained by a genre; I do it all. But I like oldies. Those are my inspirations, like Otis Redding and Jim Croce."

He had primed her heart with his charm and she was ready to be romanced by him. His good looks and smooth talk drew her to him; he serenaded her with music she had never heard before, having been raised listening to classic French songs and European pop music. He had swooped into her world, almost forcing himself into her life, and within six months, they moved in together. Within a year, Marine was pregnant. Feelings of love for Loammi had developed quickly in Marine's heart because she recognized how extraordinary he was. He was extraordinary and contradictory. On the one hand, he had a lot of talent; he was self-taught and could touch any instrument and make a melody come out of it in a matter of seconds. He could sing a song before an audience and make people howl and whistle. But on the other hand, he was not a musician that sought to appeal to the general public. He truly believed that he had been imparted a gift by God, and his mission was to preach the love and knowledge of Jesus Christ through his songs.

At that time, Marine did not have a relationship with Jesus, yet it was their discussions about God that had bound her to Loammi. While in retrospect, his habits did not particularly reflect the purity and perfection that she would have thought a man of God would exhibit, those imperfections were probably what God used to reach out to Marine. Loammi was cool. He was talented, he was his own man like no other. He was deep and simple, close and aloof, strong yet vulnerable. He was the opposite of her. He did not know how to write an academic paper, but he knew how to fix a radio. He did not know how to analyze elements of discourse or debate the theoretical constructs of postmodernism, but he knew how to share his life story with words that grip your emotions and wrench your stomach.

"Baby, do you know what it feels like, when your own brother betrays you like that? Those that you love and need that aren't there for you? I had no one in life to count on but God! Through all my mistakes in life—and I will admit, I'm not perfect, baby, I know I've made mistakes—but I know what love is and I will give anything to help my brother! If you need something and you're my friend, my family even, I will search the earth to find it. I will die for you!

"You know, baby, it's because I know that God's love has more than anyone in this world has to offer. Men judge you; they don't truly care about you. Governments compete for greed and kill entire populations, but God sets you free and gives you power to love even your worst enemy!"

At first Loammi's constant recognition of God had appealed to Marine's intellectual curiosity. She found that when he asked her questions, she wasn't quite sure what she thought, and at times it made her feel uncomfortable, as if cornered. Why was he so grounded in his beliefs, and she wasn't? How could she get to know this God he seemed to believe in so strongly?

It was when Loammi offered her a Bible on her twenty-ninth birthday, nine months after they had met, that Marine started reading the Bible for the very first time. Of course, she had read excerpts of Catholic pamphlets at church in France before; she had even attended masses where people are told to get up and sit down, then get up again, and where they are told to repeat "The Lord be with you!" and "And also with you." Marine had always thought that the Bible had to be the most boring piece of literature on earth. But Loammi said that it was the most important gift you could give a person. He said that you could lose anything in life, but if you had the Word of God, that was all that you needed. Marine always felt a pinch of anxiety when he mentioned losing everything and being all alone, because for her, the idea of having no one in life but God seemed quite scary. But because she was attracted to Loammi and the way he loved her, which was by disclosing himself very intimately and not holding back, she started reading the book of Genesis. Her Bible was signed "To my love," and her four-year-old son had even drawn a sun in it. And so it became a token of love.

At the same time as Marine was discovering the Word of God, she met a neighbor who was a fellow doctoral student at the university, and who was a Christian. She and her husband were from Hungary and lived a couple doors down from her and Loammi. Both being European expatriates in America is what started their friendship. Marine felt a sisterhood with this joyful Hungarian woman named Zsófia. They often had intense discussions about the Bible because her new friend was quite knowledgeable about Scripture. Furthermore, Zsófia did not shun her for living in sin with Loammi, which she discovered she was doing, but encouraged her to love her mate and love God. Marine started attending their church, but had shared with Zsófia that she still felt aloof from the rest of the congregation. Her friend's response had comforted her.

"You're a French woman. Of course you will always feel that you never fully belong to an American church! But this church is a very good one to give you a solid biblical foundation."

While Marine treasured her new friendship with Zsófia and started to identify with fellow Christians, she wished that Loammi would come to church with her. It was a small charismatic church led by a local pastor and his wife and a few other couples who were part of various ministries. Service was on Saturdays, because the core mission of the church was to reach and preach the gospel to students, and having service on Saturday evenings would, they hoped, keep the youth out of the bars. That church ended up being a place where Marine felt like she was part of a community, even though she also felt different from the others, who were either younger than her or were her age but had their lives together—that is, couples who had children and were married. It was in the midst of that difference that she realized that God makes everyone unique and valuable, and this challenged her to love her neighbors. She only wished Loammi would join the family.

"I'm sorry, baby. One day I will come, I promise, but you know it's so weird that this church has service on Saturday evenings. I don't want to go to church and then go to the bar. I'm a musician, that's what I do, and I'd feel like a hypocrite!"

Though Loammi was not a part of her church life, Marine could only feel her love for him growing, as did her love for Christ. The more she read the Bible, the more passionate she and Loammi felt about the Word of God, and about each other. He saw with his own eyes a transformation in her. He described the day when the Holy Spirit fell on her, saying that her countenance changed, and it was as if a light had shone on her.

Loammi was persuaded that God had brought Marine into his life to be a blessing to him; he considered her different from the American white women he had met before. There was a candor and class about her that intrigued him. For her part, Marine knew that there was a purpose to meeting Loammi and believed that God had chosen this man to be her husband: he was strong, he was good-looking, he possessed wisdom and experience. He had discernment and knowledge of the Word of God; he possessed all the characteristics of a leader who knows where to go and how to survive. He was the kind of man who would be likely to rally lost people to fight off enemies, the one likely to survive if a natural disaster overcame the world, and above all, he was the man that God had chosen to lead her to Jesus.

2

The Rebel

"Behold, to obey is better than sacrifice, and to hearken than the fat of rams. For rebellion is as the sin of witchcraft, and stubbornness is as iniquity and idolatry. Because thou hast rejected the word of the LORD, he hath also rejected thee from being king."

—1 SAM 15:22–23

SAUL WAS OFFICIALLY KING of Israel. He had charmed his people, the Israelites, with his good looks and his wisdom. Having reigned peacefully over Israel for a couple of years, he had established a military presence around his kingdom. But in the third year, he began to stir hostility with the Philistines when he made his son Jonathan's army attack their garrison in Geba. While they defeated the Philistines, that attack led to a larger battle. Without thinking strategically, and without praying to God, Saul retreated from Michmash, in the central plateau of Benjamin, to Gilgal, east of the land, which gave the enemy the chance to control that abandoned territory. Saul was starting to act rashly. Samuel, the prophet, had asked him to wait for him seven days, but the king could not keep himself together; his men were scattered and frightened, so he must also have felt afraid. Instead of waiting obediently, he decided to take matters into his own hands and give the burnt offering, which was Samuel's duty to perform. By not following the proper order, Saul ended up profaning the sacred ritual and the name of the Lord. Though he was seeking God's favor, Saul allowed the fear of his circumstances to get in the way of his obedience to God. Because he failed to place his trust in God and deliberately disobeyed him, Saul was reprimanded by Samuel. Nonetheless, God remained with the Israelites in the battle, and that day, Saul and his son Jonathan defeated the garrison of the Philistines.

However, Saul disobeyed God again: he rushed into another battle without allowing the priest who was with him to pray to God about it first. Saul's impetuous character and impatience caused him to continue to rebel against the Lord rather than grow in his knowledge. Because he was rash, he mandated a fast. By taking this action, he was subjecting his men to defeat by weakening his army. He also caused the men who had already eaten that day to sin.

Saul was convicted and admitted that those men's sinfulness was his fault. He desired to make amends with God. As a man who hurts a woman later brings her flowers to seek forgiveness, Saul sought to redeem himself and built an altar to the Lord. But God is not a woman that he can be fooled with flowers and false repentance; that night, when Saul inquired of him about going after the Philistines, God did not answer.

At that point, Saul did not realize the gravity of his sin; he had acted as a man who has confessed his sins with his lips but not his heart, and so is able to move on without remorse or restitution to those he has hurt.

Saul was acting without wisdom. He had cursed his own army by proclaiming the fast. It turned out that his own son, Jonathan, had eaten honey that day, having not been made privy to his father's fast. Consequently, God had stopped moving on behalf of the Israelites, and Saul did not understand why. When they cast lots and the lot fell on Jonathan, Saul judged him guilty and was willing to put him to death. Not only did Saul not give thought to the possibility that he was at fault for putting his own son in this predicament, but it is hard to believe that he was actually willing to have him killed. Luckily for Jonathan, Saul's counselors spoke up and Saul changed his mind as quickly as he had made it: he did not curse his son after all.

Saul's character started to change. His impulsive decision-making revealed an unstable temperament that caused him to lack discernment and violate his own word, as well as the Word of God. For a while, Saul continued to gain victory over all his enemies: the Moabites, the Ammonites, the Edomites, and the Amalekites. However, Saul only partially obeyed God's command to destroy all the Amalekites, for he let some go. It was clear to Samuel that the king was now unfit for his position.

God himself told Samuel, "it repenteth me that I have set up Saul to be king: for he is turned back from following me, and hath not performed my commandments." When Samuel confronted Saul, the latter at first insisted that he had followed the commandments of the Lord by killing the Amalekites, but Samuel reminded him that with God, the end does not justify the means, *for "obedience is better than sacrifice." He said that God had rejected Saul as king and that his kingdom would therefore end.*

Saul begged Samuel to turn again to his side so he could worship God. At first Samuel resisted him, but Saul insisted, and Samuel agreed to go with him so his failures would not be uncovered in front of his army. It is said that from that day on, Samuel no longer associated himself with Saul. The consequences of Saul's repetitive rebellions and half-hearted repentances had hurt Samuel so much that he mourned for Saul until the day of his death, and this grieved God to the point that he regretted appointing Saul. (1 Sam 13–15)

THE MORE MARINE GREW in the knowledge of Jesus, the more she started to see that Loammi was not following all the rules and codes of conduct laid out in the Word of God, and it started to bother her.

"Honey, why don't you join a church?" asked Marine.

"I guess you could say that I know God fully and I believe in Jesus Christ, but I am what they call a 'backsliding Christian,' I guess, if you want to put a name on it. Have I ever told you, baby, how I gave my life to God? I was in a group home then, and I felt I had made such a mess of my life that the only way to get it right was to turn to God completely, to give him my life fully. You know how I love music, right? Well, God doesn't want you to have any idols, and that means he doesn't want you to put anything above him. I have often wondered if the reason that I have not been successful in my career is that I have not given myself fully to it, and maybe music is not what God wants for me, at least, not the success—because in this world, the industry is so corrupt, and sometimes I feel like in order to be really successful, I'd have to sell my soul.

"Well, you see, I was at a crossroads in my life. I had been working on these tracks and was about to send them to a music agent. I had prepared everything, even done a photo shoot—those are the pictures you saw of me with long hair. I was so sleek! Everybody said I was so talented. One could say I had it all! But something was bothering me in my spirit. I had made this track, and there I was in my room, looking at all my equipment, looking at my life and what it was all about. I had just gotten into a fight with an old friend of mine, and I was reflecting on that when something made me ask myself: 'Do you love God or do you love yourself? How much do you really love him? Are you willing to give God your all?'

"That night I debated with myself; I had to prove to myself that I didn't love music more than God, and I thought that I should start doing it right away or else I would never do it. I really wanted God in my life, more than anything . . . so I started tearing up a tape. 'Oh, you're gonna feel sick in the morning!' this little voice whispered. That was the Devil trying to trick me. So, it made me even more determined and I tore up another tape; then I started tearing up my instruments. That whisper got louder: 'You're crazy, man; you're gonna be sick when you wake up and realize what you did!' But the more I tore stuff up the more I was proving to myself that I wanted God in my life more than anything!

"By the end of the night I had destroyed all my music and all my equipment. I was afraid that I would regret it in the morning, but quite the opposite: when I woke up, I felt free. I went to get myself a Bible. I walked in this Christian store and I selected myself a King James version, because I had always heard that the King James was the real Bible, and everything else was nothing more than another version, which means a distortion of the truth. It was even confirmed to me directly by God, because there was a man in the store that day who was looking at me very quietly. He came over, and we started a conversation. I sensed that something about him was not quite right. You know how God says that we should test the spirits, and that every spirit that does not confess that Jesus is God come in the flesh is not of God? Well, I asked that man: 'Do you confess that Jesus Christ came in the flesh to save us from our sins?' He nodded and everything, but when it came down to it, he would not confess. That's when I knew that he was the Devil. He was trying to get me to buy a different version of the Bible, an NIV, but I knew that what I wanted was the King James. That man was trying to get me to wander from the truth. Isn't it amazing, baby? When you give your life to God, you make the Devil mad! And so, the Devil was after me because he knew that I meant business."

Marine realized from Loammi's many lectures that he spent a lot of energy exhibiting hatred for the Devil; in fact, one could say that he hated evil with a passion, and that contradiction disturbed her. It was always there, all the while as he spoke marvelous things about God.

"So, I started walking with God. I gave myself my Bible. Actually, I like to think that God himself gave me his Word. I didn't go to a church or anything; God directly revealed himself to me. I kept my Bible on a nice piece of furniture, and I sprayed good cologne on it. It has revealed so many things to me, baby; God is so real! I felt so free, and so loved! I gave up drinking, and smoking, women, everything! I got a job at this gym, and every day I went swimming. I felt purified. Sometimes with other Christian friends, we made those posters about Jesus and we would go and slide them under people's doors."

Loammi sighed and closed his eyes, as if the memories of turning his life over to God had revived his heart.

"I was but seventeen or eighteen years old. Ah, I should never have left. The biggest mistake I've made in my life was to leave God. Don't ever leave him, baby; it's not worth it. I wish I could get it back; I don't know if I can get it back."

"Well, what happened?" asked Marine. "Why do you feel like you can't get him back?"

She had heard the story before, but she still did not understand why he was so stuck in his walk. After all, God is a god of second chances and attenuating circumstances.

"Well, you don't understand. Most people don't understand. They feel like they are worshipping God, but in fact they are not, unless they give everything to him. Most people have one foot in the Word and one foot in the world. But following Christ means to leave absolutely everything behind. That's what the apostles did."

Loammi sighed. "I tried that life but after a while, it was just too hard. One day, I went to buy a pack of cigarettes, and I started smoking again. It's just—his standards are just too high. I had been so pure and perfect; I just couldn't do it anymore. I remember telling God his standards were too high for anyone to follow!"

"Could it be that you were just too hard on yourself?" asked Marine, picking up the cigarette that Loammi passed her, letting the calming relief of nicotine fill her lungs and exhaling slowly. "I mean, what really matters is what is on the inside, isn't it? God is after your heart."

"Well, the one thing for sure is that he is real. And he says that he will never leave you nor forsake you, and I can testify that he has never left me; but I am not good enough, I have backslid, and if I ever get to the point where I get back on track with him again, baby, I swear I never want to leave him again."

Those were the times when she did not understand Loammi. For some reason, Marine had no problem being imperfect. Perhaps she should worry a bit more about *her* salvation, but God made her feel good, not bad. It was so strange that God used this man in her life who was a Christian, and yet not really. As time went on and as she herself grew in the Word of God, Marine thought that his faith was weak. While he was knowledgeable, he did not trust God. He was afraid. He did things in his own way and with his own might. He was short-tempered and quick to change his mind. He confessed to God with his lips but did not believe in the power of prayer. For example, after he prayed about something, why would he agonize over the same trouble he just gave over to God? She did not understand that! It was as if something was preventing him to give his life over to God, and Marine wanted to figure out what it was.

Truly, Loammi was two sides of one coin. On the one hand, he was an exemplary man who was intelligent and knowledgeable, talented and generous, and who had a pure and simple heart. But on the other hand, he would get discouraged quickly and, frankly, did not work that hard at making music to provide for his family, as he had promised he would. In fact, sometimes she wished that instead of dreaming about fame and glory, Loammi would say fewer words and take a little more action. Yet, Marine wanted to be supportive of his goals because she was certain he had the talent to achieve them. If that meant they would have to survive off her part-time job for a while, it was worth it. What this man needed the most was someone who believed in him. She felt this way because deep down inside, she perceived that he lacked the drive to see something through, when push came to shove, and she did not quite understand that. The road seemed clearer to her: push through, you have the talent, you can do it! After all, she was walking a similar road: alone in a strange land 6, ooo miles away from family, she felt a bit isolated at times, in spite of the many friends she had made; she never sensed that she was fully integrated. But she had a purpose and it was to finish her doctoral degree. It was simple to her, a box to check off; just do it!

THE COUPLE HAD BEEN together for almost four years. They were raising Marine's son and had a baby girl together. Marine continued to see Loammi as a fine man who possessed talent and potential, a good heart, and a great deal of biblical knowledge. In particular, she treasured the fact that God's name was mentioned on a daily basis in her household, and that their children would grow up to know the Lord. It was clear to both her and Loammi that they had embarked on a lifetime commitment and that they should get married, because after all, God hates sin, and even though they lived as husband and wife, they had yet to tie the knot.

In the time they had been together, their love for and knowledge of each other had grown to the point that they knew pretty much everything about the other, and had common values. While the way that God had brought them together was undeniable and made their story look like a fairy tale on the outside, there were times when Marine felt unsettled about Loammi's distrust of others and overprotective attitude. For example, if the worker at the drive-through got the order wrong, Loammi would murmur that he or she probably did it on purpose and had to be racist. Sometimes he would press her to ask friends for favors, such as borrowing money, and Marine did not like to do that. And other times, his behaviors were simply inappropriate and embarrassing. One afternoon, their three-year-old daughter came back from school and complained that a boy spat on her face. Loammi took the phone and called the teacher, demanding an explanation of how she could have let this happen.

"I understand that you are upset" said the pre-school teacher on the other side of the line, "and I can assure you that I have spoken to the little boy, and he will not do this again."

Loammi had retorted, "You are missing the point. What if this kid has AIDS? Do you know for sure that this child does not have AIDS? I mean, is that possible?"

Hearing him belittle the schoolteacher had made Marine feel so uncomfortable that she reached out to her the next day and apologized on his behalf.

"That's OK," the teacher responded, "he did not have his listening ears on."

The reassuring reactions of others helped Marine gain perspective and suppress her instincts. She came to the rational conclusion that Loammi had flaws, as she did herself. Being desirous of becoming the excellent servant that God had called her to be, she believed those moments were testing her faith and helped shape her character in the image of God. Thus, she became very good at riding the waves of doubt and shame when they occurred. She also found out that it could be challenging to respect her man in public, but it was a necessary trial to mold her into the perfect wife she was meant to be.

WHEN THE COUPLE FINALLY decided to get married, they drove to Chicago, where Loammi grew up, and where they had visited his family several times.

"I know that the Devil is really gonna hate me, now," said Loammi, "because I am doing God's will.

"Marriage is sacred, and that's why I've never gotten married yet—because it is so important to God. When you do God's will, it makes the Devil mad, and you can expect him to come full force after you."

While he said those words, Marine's favorite Isley Brothers's song played in the car: "Voyage to Atlantis." She closed her eyes. The high-pitched cry of the guitar pinched a cord in her heart, as the singer questioned whether he should go on without the woman he loved. The lyrics exalted the glorious city of Atlantis, personified as the love of his life, the real object of his desire. The song had a heart-wrenching, gripping anguish to it, the kind that forces you to face the possibility that romance can go wrong. Was Loammi unsure of his commitment? Was she? Why did he always seem to question everything all the time? She looked at him. He was still driving effortlessly after many hours behind the wheel, exhibiting no signs of fatigue or weakness, taking the lead as a man and taking her somewhere magical: to Chicago.

"Atlantis . . . " The song playing in the car spoke of attraction as a mag-
netic force that the singer inevitably returns to. It was a song about eternal
love. Like the city he came from, Loammi was strong. He was fierce. In spite
of the careless comments he uttered at times, Marine was learning to not hold
him to every word he said, but look at what desires those words revealed.
He knew what he wanted, and he went for it. In a sense, he was safety. He
wasn't afraid of winning or losing. He seemed to hold his own. Marine hoped
that once they were married, Loammi would start feeling more whole, that
the internalized rejection he carried from his childhood would go away, as
would his inconsistent moods, and that God would patch his holes. Likewise,
she knew that when she got married, her new family would be everything she
never had as a child: a family that truly loves one another.

This was their fourth road trip to the windy city, and it seemed that
each one had strengthened their love and solidified their bond. Chicago
was part of Loammi—a bold and thrilling metropolis conquered by love
and freedom where he was born and raised. It was also a city she had traveled to with her best friend as a teenager, so it already held a special place
in her heart. More recently, she had met Loammi's birth mother and had
felt invited into the most intimate part of Loammi's life: his beginnings, his
childhood and its dysfunctions, the source of all answers about him.

The best part about going to Chicago together was the six-hour drive.
Road trips naturally brought them closer together: listening to music, eating
gas station snacks, and talking while time stood still through the endless
highways. On the road, you are partners stuck in a car together for better
or worse. It made sense that Loammi and Marine got married in Chicago.
Loammi had met many women and would have had the opportunity to
get married earlier in life, but to him, marriage meant something. It was
a relationship blessed by God, like the coronation of a king who finds his
appointed queen. He had loved many women, but he had never felt that
God was ordaining a marriage in his life. With Marine, his relationship had
grown in a way no other had; he had observed that it was his influence that
caused her to welcome Christ into her life and change the way she thought
about certain things. He was convinced that God was behind this union.
Marine was a gift from God, and with her by his side, he knew that he would
be blessed, because God answered her prayers. She was like a lifeline between him and God.

For Marine, they were already a family, having two children and a
common passion for Jesus, so it was time to honor God and marry the man
she loved. Both of them had had an unconventional start, but God in his
loving kindness had brought them together to experience love and family
under his banner, and she did not want to make any more mistakes in life.

She was ready to be a wife and love her husband and children. It was time the fairy tale truly began.

Their love story certainly had elements of a fairy tale, such as the way they felt about each other, how often Loammi told her he loved her, and how she was able to make him feel good about himself, as if she had special powers to calm him down when he struggled. But there were some disturbing and strangely ominous moments as well.

THEY WERE MARRIED IN a small church in Chicago, and returned home feeling galvanized. Loammi felt like God had covered him with a shield and would protect his life from now on. In a sense, being married changed nothing, yet it changed everything. They both loved to call each other "my husband" and "my wife," and they cherished wearing wedding rings. For Loammi, it was the first time that he ever wore a ring on his finger, and that made him feel like he was a new man. He never took it off, except when necessary; one time, a week after they were married, he took it off temporarily for Marine to give him a hand massage. She carefully placed it in a box that her mother had sent her in the mail that same day, and which contained various pieces of fantasy jewelry, to keep it safe. After the massage they fell asleep, and when they woke up, they forgot about the ring. Marine put away the jewelry box she had just received.

The next day, Loammi realized that his ring was not on his finger. He panicked. He looked everywhere in the house but to no avail. He wondered, did it fall off when he was working outside a few days before? Or when he was running errands? He thought he had heard a small sound of metal when he got out of the car . . . Marine looked everywhere as well, having completely forgotten about the box of jewelry her mother had sent. Loammi was getting depressed, and Marine knew that his depression was often the first step to getting angry. She dreaded the estranged and ugly ogre that took over the face of her beautiful prince, which she knew so well. Fortunately, one of his friends reassured him that the ring was not what made him a married man, and he could easily buy another one, since it was just a plain band anyway. Marine thanked God for friends like that who knew how to look at the bright side of things, and that day Loammi calmed down. Yet, she knew somehow that he would not be at peace forever, because he typically was not able to take bad news well without eventually bursting out in anger. And sure enough, the moment came.

She was in the kitchen getting ready to make dinner. The ogre came down and stared at her with his angry eyes.

"So, let me ask you, why did you marry me, really?"

"What do you mean? I married you because I love you!"

"But look, we haven't been married for very long, and the Devil is already starting to curse me. He took my wedding ring away, and he must be laughing!"

"Honey, I'm very sorry about that, and I've looked everywhere. I really hope that we can find it, but if not, we can buy another one. Or maybe we'll find it when we're not thinking about it."

"What do you care? You didn't lose your ring. You're not the one that's cursed. In fact, you're good now; you got your green card! So now, you can stay in this country and be good; you don't need me. Maybe that's why you married me; you're all set now!"

"What are you saying? I love you. You're my husband, my everything!"

Loammi stepped back and grabbed Marine's Bible, then threw it at her. "You don't love me!"

Watching her precious Bible fly open and crash flat against the kitchen cabinet made Marine feel like she had been hit in the stomach. As if she had been knocked down with the Bible, she shrunk and slid down against the wall, confused and sobbing.

"Oh yeah, you can cry, but I'm the one who is cursed, and you are no different than anybody else!"

Loammi kept talking for what seemed like an hour. At the end, Marine was devastated and drained of energy. She went to bed, rescuing and taking her Bible with her. When she woke up the next day, she experienced the same feeling she did when something like that happened: What happened? Did that really happen? The man waking up next to her was so different from the one who had yelled at her the night before; it was confusing to think that this husband, who was now in his right mind, had lashed out at her and acted crazy. It also seemed that once Loammi had let go of his fear or anger, albeit in destructive ways, he was able to move on. Though it hurt her feelings, his arguments seemed to be his coping mechanism for personal problems, and eventually, he did not mean the bad things he said.

Things calmed down and life continued.

UNFORTUNATELY, LOAMMI PERSISTED TO put stumbling blocks in his own path, adding unnecessary difficulty to his life. He had a proud spirit that caused him to hate bending to rules and regulations. This was especially so when it came to the systems in power, which he thought were wicked and oppressive. He was in the habit of driving late at night, to and from various places where he met other musician friends, sometimes to network, sometimes to hang out.

One night, Marine was awakened by a phone call at two in the morning.

"Baby, it's me. Uh, the police pulled me over."

"What?"

"Yeah. They said we have a taillight out, but I don't believe that; you know how they are. Anyway, I've been drinking, so they're gonna take me, but I got them to let me leave the car on the street, at least, so you can go get it in the morning before they impound it."

"Are you serious?"

This was not the first time that Marine was interrupted from her sleep. Sometimes she wondered if her life with Loammi was going to include constant surprises like this. She had just finished studying and gotten to bed an hour earlier! If it wasn't something dramatic, it was Loammi needing to talk, or needing her to listen to his music. Now she had to figure out how to get to where he had left the car, which was closer to downtown than the outskirts where they lived. She would probably have to request a ride from a friend and make arrangements according to someone else's timetable. Marine did not like to have to depend on others when the favors needed were the result of Loammi's poor choices. She was again embarrassed by his conduct, and those moments tested the honor that God said a woman should give her husband. Marine certainly felt that she was doing her fair share of covering for Loammi's sins, and naturally, she resented that. Yet, she tried to justify to herself that times such as those forced her to push through her natural discomfort and allowed her to nourish a selfless nature. Loving and honoring her husband when he clearly did wrong was a trial that taught her to lean on the love of the Holy Spirit within her.

After this incident, Loammi's license was suspended, but he continued to drive. What a way to make things more complicated!

"Honey, you should just deal with it, pay the fine, do the classes, and be done with it."

"Our money is better spent in other places; besides, I'm not bowing down to this racist system. They will continue to pull me over for no reason anyway."

To Loammi's credit, it was true that the justice system was permeated with racism. However, Marine feared things would get worse if he continued to refuse to follow the rules.

"Rules don't apply to me!" he had said once. "I am bound by no man's rules and no system. I'm my own man. I obey no man but God."

In the meantime, he did have a suspended license, and that was not going to help them. Marine started to fear that their life together would bring added insecurities.

3

The Depressed Personality

"Come unto me, all ye that labour and are heavy laden, and I will give you rest.
Take my yoke upon you, and learn of me; for I am meek and lowly in heart: and
ye shall find rest unto your souls. For my yoke is easy, and my burden is light."

—MATT 11:28–30

SINCE SAUL HAD REBELLED against him repeatedly, the Lord God of Israel declared him unfit for the position of king. He told Samuel that he would anoint
another to be king over Israel, and that this time, he would select a man based
on the character of his heart, not on his stature. So, the Lord God selected David,
a shepherd who was the youngest and frailest son of Jesse. Per God's instruction,
Samuel anointed David with oil in Bethlehem, unbeknownst to Saul.

Though God had disqualified Saul, he did not kill him right away; in
fact, it took about thirteen years for God to bring Saul's reign to an end and
for David to ascend to the throne. However, it says that when God rejected
Saul, God removed his Spirit from Saul, and tormented him with an evil spirit.
From that moment on, King Saul experienced various emotional and psychological troubles.

Saul's servants sought to comfort their king and alleviate his pain. They
had heard of a man who knew how to play the harp. Perhaps back then,
around 1050 BC, music was already used as an antidepressant. Saul's men
certainly believed that the gentle sound of a harp would heal Saul's troubled

mind, for they told their king about this shepherd anointed by God, whose name was David, the son of Jesse the Bethlehemite. Saul sent for him.

When David arrived at the palace, he found favor before the king. Saul asked his father Jesse to let David come live in his palace and serve him, and so David dwelled with Saul, who made him his armor bearer. David quickly gained the trust of the king through his good work and his loyalty. He served Saul faithfully, and when the evil spirit tormented Saul's mind, David took his harp and played until Saul could breathe again and was relieved of what was most likely a psychotic episode. (1 Sam 16)

LOAMMI HAD TROUBLE RESTING. He wasn't sure why he was feeling this way all of a sudden. He had received bad news, and the disappointment of an opportunity that was suddenly unavailable brought to the surface a cumulation of other feelings about things that had not lived up to his expectations, however realistic or not, and however grave or not. The fact was that he could not shake it off. He had been fretting for almost three days, sitting in the dark, and getting up only to eat, drink, and use the bathroom. The shades were closed in the bedroom and darkness claimed its territory.

"Honey, why not let me open the window? It's so dark in here; no wonder you're not feeling well. Look outside, the sunlight is so bright and it smells so good."

Loammi tugged the bed cover over his head. "No, leave it alone, please. You go outside, you and the kids."

Having heard their names, the children ran into the bedroom to show their angelic faces.

"Are we going outside?"

"Dad, can we play at the big playground?" asked their little girl.

"Dad, can we fly my kite today? It's windy, and you said next time there's enough wind, we'll fly the kite," their son insisted simultaneously.

Loammi lifted his head up and took a pitiful look at his children.

"Guys, I'm feeling really tired. Your mom is going to take you. We'll all go another time, I promise."

Knowing from experience to not hold the word "promise" to its literal interpretation, the children sighed and ran out of the bedroom.

Loammi begged Marine to leave him alone.

"I just need to shake this feeling off me. It has nothing to do with you, and there's nothing you can do. Please go. You and the kids should enjoy this beautiful day. Don't worry about me."

Marine could not help but worry about her husband. She hated the days when he got in those moods, sometimes for no apparent reason. What she resented, in reality, was not his malady, but rather the fact that it did not make sense to her. Loammi's problems were not insurmountable. Losing an opportunity to play a gig, dealing with car problems or money problems— that was not the end of the world. Problems were meant to be fixed and she wanted to fix her husband's problems. If he would at least go see a doctor, it would help. Instead, he chose to do nothing. She wanted to help him, and she contemplated solutions, but he would not be helped. It wrenched her heart. It was strange to go to the park, play with her children, and chit-chat with the neighbors knowing that her husband was not well. She wondered to what extent the kids were affected by their dad's strange behavior, if they had learned to navigate around his ways as she had and pretend to ignore the elephant in the room. On the outside, they appeared to be genuinely happy running around the playground. Normal children. They talked to other children and shared their cookies. Life as a gift from God seemed beautiful on the outside, and so that was what Marine chose to focus on.

They returned home before dusk, and Marine's heart sank within her when she saw that their side of the townhouse, which stood in the dark, was also pitch black on the inside. It was only 6 p.m., but it looked like it was the middle of the night. She knew this would be a long night. Loammi did not speak a word, and although she tried to rub his head and shoulders, he did not return her touch. He felt cold and forlorn.

With time she had learned that these episodes, which were few and far between, would go away on their own within three days at the most, so she developed the ability to disregard them.

As TIME WENT BY, Loammi was not accomplishing any of the goals he had set for himself, and playing music had become a series of inconsistent gigs, not a career path. He did spend most of his time by his recorder, creating songs and melodies, but he did not collaborate to create a music label, which was his dream. Nothing he pursued seemed to bear fruit; he would take one step forward and three backward. He got his family's hopes up and let them down just as quickly.

"Guess who I met last night, babe?," he announced one day, coming back from a music fair. "This producer, he worked with this singer! I ran into him last night and he gave me his card! I'm going to call him, and I'm sure he'll have something for me!"

But nothing ever came of any of his plans, his promises, or his hopes. Wanting to be supportive, Marine avoided pushing him too much, or even discussing a topic that would upset him. She even omitted to tell him when an unexpected bill came, because she found it easier to deal with fears and problems on her own. She knew that she could deal with them herself and find solutions before taking the chance of worrying her husband. Perhaps it was because of Loammi's angry moods, which made everyone feel uneasy. Gradually, she told him less and less, afraid to wake up the beast and push his buttons by bringing up problems. So, she placed her cares at the feet of Jesus.

"Lord, please," she asked in faith, "heal my husband. You have plans for his life; please see that they are accomplished in your time. As you forgive my sins, forgive his as well, and help him hear your voice."

Loammi liked to watch Marine read her Bible and pray. He said she reminded him of his grandma, who was the godliest woman he had ever known. Marine's quiet and poised countenance in the face of adversity brought a sense of peace to him. Sometimes he would taunt her and argue just to see how far he could go until she got fed up. After all, he knew that she was not perfect, and did not always listen to him, which drove him crazy; as if she thought she knew it all with her educated ways! But deep down, he knew that she was a good woman, a good wife and a good mother. Most days. Because there were days when she acted as if she purposely did the opposite of what he wanted, as if she had not learned anything from what he tried to teach her! He hated those moments when he felt separated from her, as if she was able to hold her own without him.

"Babe, I am you, and you are me," he loved to say.

Marine never understood exactly what he meant when he said that, because the syntax was clearly wrong, and she tended to take things literally. *I am you* was a linguistic impossibility. It was also clear that they were very different in their makeups, their characters and their upbringings. She could not possibly ever think like him. But like most things she did not understand about her husband, she preferred to put it out of her mind and focus on what she could do, which was display her love and affection for him and their children, go to work (somebody had to go to work!), and take care of her home. In no way was she going to have a family life like the one she grew up in, with her parents, in France; love in her household would make itself known and triumph over everything!

On this side of the Atlantic, family time was precious. Marine and Loammi liked to walk through nature with their children, play in public parks, eat ice cream, and go to fun places like the zoo or swimming pools. Marine treasured these moments, yet on some level she sensed that her children were troubled by the same underlying fear that developed in her: that Daddy was not fully happy, and that at any time he could switch from being fun and loving to cold and angry.

So, she tried her best to help him, to be the healing touch that he needed to conquer his demons. Because she loved God, and he spoke to her through the reading of his Word, through sermons, and through her Christian friends—because his Spirit within her moved her heart and ministered to her soul—she found the strength and the joy to deal with it all, and to be content with where God had placed her. She knew that with Loammi, it was just a matter of time until he would accomplish great things for God, and his musical talent would bear fruit. If only he stopped getting mad for no reason!

EVIDENTLY, WHEN HE WAS at his best—that is, himself—Loammi possessed the ability to control himself and walk away when he was upset. But sometimes, when he was in his odd moods, it was as if demons started tormenting him, and he acted out in strange, sometimes scary ways. What Marine dreaded the most was not being hurt by him–after all, he had never hit her. Well, perhaps a dark look or a shove here and there, but that wasn't really hitting. She wasn't truly scared of him or anything like that. It was just mentally draining to stay up all night listening to long and senseless arguments. There was also another concern: his depression made him drink, and it was possible that the drinking made him act irrationally. These behaviors became more and more frequent as time went by.

"You know, have you ever noticed that sometimes, there are things in your spirit that I notice?" he said one evening after dinner.

"What are you talking about?"

"You know what I mean. You act like you don't understand what I'm saying. You, Ms. PhD, is this too much for you? Is this too intelligent for you, Mrs. Doctor? Does it go above your head?"

"I'm sorry, I really have no idea what you are talking about, and I'd like to understand. Did I do something to upset you? Can you give me an example of what you are talking about?"

Loammi sighed. He stared at her blankly.

"I know what I see in you; you can't fool me."

Marine knew that there was no point in responding to those incoherent exhortations, and no winning them, but sometimes a point of pride in her, the remnant of her old self, had to respond and play the game; it was not as if her husband would leave her alone anyway. So, she addressed his thought process as if trying to deconstruct the theory of an author, and find the irrefutable point that would end the discussion! Each time she did so, she won the argument. Unfortunately, life is not lived in reality as it is on paper, and on some level, Marine knew those behaviors were not normal. In fact, at times they made her wonder what it would be like to be trapped by a psychopath and monitor every word that came out of her mouth in order to save herself. That was a fearful thought, and her imagination had a way of getting the best of her sometimes. The reality was that Loammi was a man with a heart and feelings, with a will to love and do right, and Marine loved him. She loved him and saw that he was tormented, so she wanted to help, but did not know what to do with his undercurrents.

She decided that if she loved the Lord, she should not let fear stand in the way of her faith. After all, "God has not given us a spirit of fear," read Second Timothy. So, she trusted God to intervene and calm Loammi's irrational mind. This time, Loammi let go of the dispute. A few hours later, he was back to himself.

"Do we have any aspirin? I've had a headache for hours! I will see a dentist in the morning, but this hurts too much!"

Marine knew that he would not let her sleep if she did not find a way to help him. She took his head in her hands, caressed his cheek, and prayed over him. "Father, thank you for healing this toothache, since the dentist is closed right now. Take it away, please, take away the hurt." In her heart she was praying that God would take away his sickness.

"Wow, honey, when you prayed at first the pain intensified, and then it went away, and now it is completely gone!"

"Praise the Lord!" she whispered. "I am going to sleep."

"Baby, I love you. God loves you. I have an amazing wife!"

"I love you too. Goodnight. We'll talk in the morning."

Marine hesitated to get into a discussion with her husband about his irrational behaviors. It was strange to her that he could so quickly forget that he had hurt her feelings just a few minutes earlier, and yet he genuinely meant what he said. To her, the two feelings expressed in his subsequent conversations were such opposites that she thought that one had to display his real sentiments, and the other something he did not mean. Therefore, in trying to perfect the skill of understanding her husband, Marine progressively learned to disregard the words and even the behaviors that were contrary to an expression of love. Because she knew without the shadow of a doubt that her husband loved her very deeply, she was able, or perhaps simply willing, to ignore what came to her in forms of unexpected criticism, insults, or anger, viewing it as the voice of the enemy as opposed to the voice of God. Likewise, she came to hold on to the words that Loammi uttered and the actions he exhibited when they were loving and kind, as the true voice and character of her husband whom she knew loved her. This knowledge helped her tamp down her own dissident nature that was so easily offended, and as much as she could, she took her anger to God in prayer rather than picking a fight.

Loammi, meanwhile, saw in his wife's compliant nature a confirmation of God's approval of himself. She made him feel good about himself, and when he felt good about himself, he also felt validated by God. The Lord was a good god who did not keep scores of your faults, but erased them at the feet of the cross, washed them with the blood of Jesus, and forgave quickly. Loammi knew that if his wife loved him, he had to be a good man, and that understanding made him want to be an even better man—to give her the love she truly deserved.

More often than not, Loammi was in his right mind. For example, one late afternoon, he took their son out for a bike ride. A few hours later, when Marine heard their voices, she thought about putting her books down and getting dinner started. When she walked in the kitchen, she smelled a mix of beef and burned oil.

"Look, Mom, I'm helping Dad make tacos!" shouted her son proudly.

Marine smiled. That was the normal Loammi: the dad who loved playing with his kids, who made burnt food, who did the laundry without asking and unintentionally shrunk a shirt or two . . . the husband who told her how much he loved her, who left beautiful love notes by the door, who spent hours laughing with friends over the phone, who fed strangers, who brought home a bag full of candy and other unhealthy food just to put a smile on his children's faces. The man who talked about God.

"Why is God three people, Dad?"

"Well, my son, there is really one God, but he is three in one. He is the Father, that means our father, and that's why when we pray, we say "Father." He is also the Son, and that's Jesus Christ. And then he is also the Holy Spirit. God is just mysterious; he is a mysterious God who works in mysterious ways, and that's why he is so awesome."

When their son turned seven years old, they were only able to find a couple of friends who could spend the day with him. Because their son's birthday came the day after Christmas, Marine gave up trying to throw a birthday party since she knew no one would come. This year, there were three boys in the house, and she had made a cake and drawn a Spider-Man image on it, but unfortunately that was the extent of her contribution, and the boys were getting bored. Loammi stopped what he was working on to find something to entertain them. He took them outside and ended up spending the entire afternoon with them; he dug up the camping gear and set up a tent with them. Marine was impressed by his compassion and his patience. He was generous with his time and resources with all children, not just his own. Loammi had explained to her that he did not have much growing up; he suffered from not having the same toys that other kids at his school or in his neighborhood had. For Christmas, he used to pore over catalogs that his family received in the mail. He always dreamed that maybe that year, somehow, his grandma would find a way to get him one of the toys that he had circled in the catalog and left by her bedside. Unfortunately, it never happened. Marine had tried to picture his disappointment; the poor little boy must have had his feelings hurt so many times! Was his grandma able to comfort him with hugs and kisses? Did he accept and understand the injustice of his family's economic situation, or did resentment build in him?

Whatever the case, Loammi's love for their children and care for their protection was a trait that represented the best of him. His heart went out to people in need and in distress. He was the kind of man who was the first to stop and help a stranded soul, and he was quick to give his own shirt if someone asked it of him. His generosity often made Marine reconsider her own heart. For her, it required battling her own nature to sacrifice for others. She was selfish and had to think about doing what was right and good in God's eyes. Every time Loammi asked her if she had a few dollars on her to give this poor man over there, her first thought was always to worry about how much money they would have left until her next paycheck. Certainly, Loammi's attitude toward money was sometimes reckless, but in those cases his heart was in the right place. He was a spender, because he valued love over gain.

And yet there was also the abnormal side of him: the once-in-a-blue-moon unsettling person who inevitably showed up now and then, and whom both Marine and her children had come to expect intermittently.

LOAMMI HAD BEEN CHRONICALLY depressed for the last month. He got in the habit of leaving the house at nighttime and drowning his sorrows at the bar. One early morning, he came home extremely drunk. It was about 5 a.m., and he had this look that Marine recognized as "danger eyes." He was angry. He had been fighting with one of his friends at the bar. He talked about this and that, how his friend was a traitor; and then he talked about killing him. What truly scared Marine were the words that he used:

"Death is coming," he mumbled under his breath, while he was falling asleep. "I can taste the blood."

It seemed as if this was not a man talking, with cognitive abilities, but something else, a demonic force that terrified Marine; so, she waited until he fell asleep, and then she waited some more. Loammi had never physically attacked her, and perhaps she was overreacting; once he sobered up, he would be in his right mind. Marine peeked at her husband who was now fast asleep, his eyes shut, his nostrils opening and closing. Then he suddenly coughed and his eyes opened for a few seconds. His mouth twisted and words came out of it as it opened up:

"I'm just gonna close my eyes for a minute, and then I'm gonna go get this m*#&@!"

Marine was unsettled. She hated the feeling of being confused when her husband's conduct was almost insane, in spite of the love she felt for him. Should she be alarmed? Should she let it pass? Why couldn't she make up her mind? Sometimes she wished the weird and crazy things could disappear on their own, just by blinking her eyes.

The children had woken up. She walked to their bedroom and whispered softly into their little faces:

"Hey sweeties, let's be very quiet so we can let Daddy sleep. We're going to go somewhere and have fun today, OK?"

She had made up her mind. She told herself that whatever was going on in her husband's mind when he woke up, she did not want the children or herself to deal with it. It sounded dangerous: talking about killing someone was serious matter. Loammi was not well, so she should take the kids and leave the house. Since they did not have a car at that time, she called a friend from church, Linda. Linda was a remarkable woman, full of wisdom. Marine knew that if she asked for her help, she would have to disclose some information and share her concerns about her husband, and she felt that she was prepared for that crossroads.

When Linda picked her up, it felt like the door of heaven opened up to let her and her kids in. Linda had such a calming spirit that her mere presence washed away the weight Marine was carrying on her shoulders as soon as she got into the car. They took the children to a park with a sprinkler so they could play while the two women had a conversation. This is exactly what family life should feel like, thought Marine, watching other families at the park—a stable peace. After she disclosed to Linda the problems that Loammi was having, and her concerns about his behaviors, Linda was more understanding than Marine would have thought. She told Marine that her own father was an alcoholic, and that she knew the rage that accompanies a drinking man. She added that her mother never left her father, but that she did have to separate a few times, because if it got dangerous, it was time to leave.

"Did your dad ever change?"

"In time he stopped drinking. He was always difficult, but in time he got better. My mother just knew that he was her mission. She also knew two things: to leave when it was time, and to not give him access to her bank account. He didn't like that, but he couldn't do anything about it."

Loammi called.

"Honey, I've been worried about you! I'm so sorry, was I drunk? Are you guys OK?"

Marine knew from the tone of his voice that Loammi was back to himself and it was safe to go home. She thought about what Linda had said, and could identify with her mother, because she also felt that Loammi was her purpose. Her mission, even—that was a good word. Linda's mother must have been a strong woman. Perhaps God would hear her prayers as he heard those of Linda's mother. She knew that the Lord loved Loammi and wanted to deliver him from his torment.

WEEKS WENT BY. DUSK was setting in and it was time to make dinner. What a sense of peace the routine of feeding children brings to a home. The night would allow for quiet study time, accompanied by the comforting pounding on keys and strings coming through the wall, the sound that Loammi was working, and that all was well.

"What the *&%#!"

Oh no, what's going on now? thought Marine. She was afraid all this thumping and banging would disturb the neighbors. Every little problem did not have to feel like a crisis, but that seemed to be so with Loammi. This time his mixer gave out and it was the worst thing ever, because it was just one more thing to discourage him. "The Devil!" Loammi would say. Always trying to stop him from success! So, Marine would spend a good part of the night listening to his rantings and whining and groaning, and then calm the beast with words of wisdom until the power of the Holy Spirit had its way with him. Loammi wanted to provide, he wanted to be a good man, and in many ways, he was. But it was evident that there was something else in the way, perhaps a lack of faith, perhaps something deeper. He had had a hard life and he was not the man of God he wanted to be, but Marine could see that man in him. She was his wife; he was her husband. God used him to bring her to Christ, surely. God would use her to bring Loammi back to God. It just made sense.

And so, their life together went on, with each ray of sunlight promising the glory of God, each breath of fresh wind strengthening the ties of love, each child's laughter warming the heart of a mother. Life was good. It was not easy, but Marine had a dedicated love for the man she had married. In her intellect, depression became another weapon the enemy used to attack her husband, and she refused to fear the Devil over the Lord Almighty God; in time she learned how to ride those tempests, and tame the beast.

"It's me and you against the world" was Loammi's mantra. "You are my everything. You're the cure to everything that's wrong with me. God knew that it would take someone like you and someone like me to overcome this world. You are my wife; you are my everything. You heal me. The Devil doesn't want to see God win. He comes to steal, to kill, and to destroy. But together we can overcome anything."

4

The Narcissist

"...for God resisteth the proud and giveth grace to the humble."

—1 Pet 5:5

Since David had found favor in Saul's eyes, the king made him his confidant and his helper. The Word of God says that Saul trusted David because David was loyal and upstanding. He was also brave and gained popularity when he defeated the giant Goliath. Goliath was a nine-foot-tall Philistine who had threatened to enslave the Israelites, but no one in Saul's army was brave enough to fight him because of his intimidating stature. The Philistines had gathered their army to wage war against Israel, so it was imperative that the Israelites fight Goliath; his size, his full steel suit of armor, and his lance intimidated Saul's entire army, but not David.

Now, David was not a man of war—he was actually rather small in stature—but he was filled with indignation to see this uncircumcised man, meaning a Gentile, insult God's chosen people. So, he volunteered to fight the Philistine. At first, Saul had pity on him, because he was so frail and inexperienced that Saul assumed he would quickly die at the hands of the giant. But David insisted that he had fought lions and bears, and he believed that the Lord God was with him. And so it was that little David slew Goliath the giant with a sling and one stone, and of course, with God's favor.

King Saul must have been impressed by David's bravery, faith, and victory. Of course, he himself was used to winning battle after battle; he had *exhibited great pride in his own victories against the Amorites, the Amalekites, and the Philistines. At that point, Saul must have viewed David as an excellent addition to his army. So, King Saul promoted David to the position of soldier.*

Since David dwelled in Saul's kingdom and was a good and valiant man, Saul liked him. It even says in the Word of God that Saul "loved" him. Yet, a stronger friendship formed between David and Saul's son, Jonathan, for it says that Jonathan loved David as a brother. In contrast, Saul loved David because David reflected well. David was a good and loyal servant who had favor with God. He succeeded everywhere Saul sent him, and was liked by all of Saul's court. He pleased his king with his obedience and his success on the battlefield, so the king loved him with a self-centered, narcissistic kind of love. It says that Saul never let David go back to his father's house. David had actually become Saul's property, as a wife is viewed as the property of a narcissistic husband. (1 Sam 17—18:5)

LOAMMI WAS WATCHING HIS wife fold laundry. She looked like a reed frail in appearance, but not easy to uproot. Her confidence before adversity astounded him. How could she not worry about all the problems in their lives? In the world? Sometimes she had such a careless attitude, it was out of this world. "What, do you think that life is a day in the park?" he'd ask her. Or again, "Do you live in la-la land?" Perhaps France was this wonderful, perfect place to live, where crime and racism and oppression did not exist, as in this country, and she had not had to deal with all the pressures he had had to. She did mention having a difficult childhood and not being close to her father, or something like that. Come to think of it, he wasn't really sure what she had against her dad. He seemed to be a fine man according to Loammi; he was a provider, and that in itself was a huge achievement for a man in this day and age. Loammi himself was struggling to take care of his family; it would be a dream come true for him if he could one day provide for his own. If Marine did not know how hard her father must have worked, shame on her!

What was sure was that Marine must have lived a perfectly sheltered life back in France, because it was not second nature for her to worry about her surroundings. She would not have survived in the inner city like he did. No way. If he wasn't there, she'd be opening the door to strangers and getting everyone killed! She'd definitely burn the house down with her carelessness. Loammi remembered the time before they lived together, when she had stepped outside of her house to greet a neighbor, and forgot that she had a pot of water boiling on the stove! If he hadn't been there, her careless chit-chat would have caused a fire. Thank God he was there to save her from herself and keep her and his children safe. He was the man. He was very lucky to have his wife, but she was equally lucky to have him. They were made for each other.

Something else that Loammi admired about Marine was that she worked late in the evenings to prepare for her doctoral defense. She was studying literature and theory of some sort, perhaps about the West Indies. Yes, he must be right, it was something like that. Anyway, it had something to do with French. How easy it must have been to study something about your own language, come to think of it; a doctoral degree must really not be all that challenging. Regardless, he loved to watch her study, because she was a hard worker and it made him feel proud to have a wife who worked as hard as he did. It was quite often that he would pull an all-nighter himself to finish a tune or equalize a sound. Or again, to take apart a whole computer that had a virus or fix a broken recorder. God knows there was always something broken around here, and he was the fixer of everything!

So, Loammi was lucky to have a wife he truly deserved, the kind that worked hard. She cooked, she cleaned, she played with the kids, she did laundry, she taught, she studied; she did it all! She helped with the kids' homework. Well, after all, Mrs. Professor-to-be, that was a given; why would anyone expect him to be the homework supervisor? It would be against all common sense! Thank goodness she liked to socialize so she could go to the kids' school and chat with the neighbors, take their little girl outside to play, and make sure no stranger approached the kids—especially the baby, the girl, who needed constant supervision and care. With all the instructions he had given Marine over the years, she had finally gotten all those rules down and was now trustworthy in all she did.

It made sense that his wife took care of all those things, seeing as she had all the time in the world. She taught two classes a week, and the rest of the time she was home studying. What an easy gig! Not like him, who had to spend hours and hours working on music, and on top of all the problems he had had recently, with the law and all, not having a license anymore. It seemed that problems followed him—persecution, even, just like the apostles were always persecuted. The mark of a man truly special in God's eyes.

But as for her, on the other hand, his wife, it seemed that she had not a care in the world. What had totally blown Loammi's mind was the way that she had completely turned around her life when he introduced her to God. She studied the Bible diligently, prayed, and went to church. It seemed that God was really working on her: she became more patient, more respectful, less self-centered. Well, she certainly was still far from perfect—what true Christian would smoke and drink wine? It annoyed him that she picked up some of his bad habits, it would be better for her if she just followed what he said and not what he did.

"I gave you God!" he would tell her, so she'd never forget who the source of her conversion was.

WHILE GOD WASN'T ALWAYS with him—which made sense because he wasn't always following all of God's rules—the Lord was certainly with his wife. It seemed that he answered every single one of her prayers!

"With the way God answers you, you should pray that we win the lottery! He'd probably tell you in a dream all the right numbers to select!"

By the way, he didn't know why she had not taken that suggestion seriously; that was a shame not to at least try. But, she clearly had her own relationship with God, and after all, God came first, as he was supposed to. He told her all the time to never put anyone before God, not even him, so in that she was doing the right thing. Maybe God did not want him to win the lottery anyway—maybe he wanted him to struggle, like all the true men of God in Scripture struggled, not like those fake prosperity preachers nowadays and those fake churches where when push comes to shove, they never help you. Oh, Loammi had met many a homeless man who was much more generous, kind, loyal and godly than any pastor in those so-called churches. For sure the real church was on the streets; that's where the true people of God were! Jesus had always shown that.

So, that's why he never went to church with Marine. She had asked and asked, and he did go once. He made the effort. He was kind enough to give her what she wanted, but came to find out it was no different than any other white American church he had experienced. But, if it helped her, it was good that someone in the family went to church. She'd just better not expect him to go back. She had to understand him by now.

In spite of the fact that she did not understand enough of his culture, where he came from, and why life in America is harder for Black people— you would think that with studying Caribbean literature, she'd already know all that, but again, that's what those lofty white people with their high degrees learn, just words—Marine was destined for success as an educated white woman. She would make a lot of money, and that was a great safety net to have in case his music did not work out. But that was not the reason why he married her. Marine was truly the woman that God had chosen to be his wife. With all the women he had been with in his life, he hadn't met anyone as godly as she was. Oftentimes, her optimistic attitude in the face of negative circumstances or the words of wisdom she spoke when he needed to hear from God reminded him of his grandma.

"My wife is the godliest woman after grandma!" he had told his brother.

She was a beautiful, faithful woman, a PhD student, a doctor to be! Whenever he could, he loved to brag about his wife.

"I have the best wife in the world!" he would tell her. "Baby, people can't believe what an amazing wife I have! They can't believe that someone like me would have such a beautiful and perfect wife, from France, even! And you know what? They hate me for it. They don't understand how I can have the best wife! They are so jealous!"

Marine knew he was exaggerating, and it embarrassed her that he would talk like that. In all honesty, she was just a normal person, perhaps pretty—she certainly had a nice figure, she had attractive qualities—but there were so many women who were much better looking and more talented. Sometimes she did wonder why Loammi loved her. If it wasn't God who had brought them together, and his love that sustained them, they would probably not have lasted long as a couple. She often wondered if he would be happier with someone who was more remarkable, like one of those cool spoken-word artists in clubs, or those beautiful singers and background dancers he mingled with at his gigs. She wasn't all that, but he did love her, and she loved that about him. In spite of his flaws, he held God's standards very high in his heart, and he upheld the sacred bond of marriage as something never to be broken.

"Marriage is a relationship between a man, a woman, and God. Can't nobody get in between that!"

Truly, God had spoken to her heart early in their relationship, when they were still living in sin, and had taught her to develop the qualities that would make her a good wife; he had shown her—she was certain—that Loammi would be her husband. And indeed, Loammi, who thought that he would never get married, married her. He took a chance because he loved her, and he believed that she was sent to him by God; though he did not trust any man or woman, he trusted God.

Marine realized their marriage had its ups and downs; her husband was not an easy man to please, but he was like no one else. He was handsome, of course; she liked how the hair of his nostrils tickled his upper lip when he made a puzzled face. She loved to feel the hard-as-steel sensation when she grabbed his arms, which she did often, to remember that her man was her knight in shining armor. The children also had perfect confidence that should anyone come after the family, their dad would protect them. "My dad can beat up anyone!" their son bragged to his friends. Loammi was, in fact, the strongest man any of them had known, and he had enough fight stories to boast about it!

Yet, he had intense emotions; he was often hot or cold, but he had a big heart. Sometimes he was too extreme in his compliments, and Marine did not think they were realistic, but she certainly preferred to be called the best wife in the world than the Devil. Loammi carried his pain like a prisoner carries his chain: always lurching forward, first one leg, then the other. It was there when he cried, and it was there when he laughed. His love was deep in words, as deep as Loammi could go.

"I love you, honey. I've never had anything like that in my life: you are mine and I am yours. I'm all yours, baby, and you're all mine!"

WHAT ATTRACTED HER TO her husband was not the fact that he was a handsome and talented musician—though he liked to claim that he was the most coveted man in his youth, and women often found him quite attractive ("What an amazing guy!" their neighbor had said). The reason she fell for him was that deep down inside Loammi was an unpretentious man who liked the simple pleasures in life. He loved watching nature shows with their son; he taught him how to set up a tent and make a fire from scratch, how to ride a bike, how to fish, and how to change a tire. He had even tried to teach her.

"Honey, really, thank you," she had laughed, "I understand the mechanics, but look at my arms. I'm a woman; I'll never be able to crank that wrench that tight!"

It was quite incredible to see the talents Loammi possessed: he could figure out anything, such as how to take a computer apart and put it back together, arrange furniture in the way that made the most sense and occupied the least amount of space, pick up a tune in a song by listening to the first two seconds, dance, repeat French sounds perfectly, tell stories and talk about God in a way that made you want to know him.

One thing that did not make sense was the fact that with all his talent, Loammi had not made much of his life. Yes, he had told her all about his plights, the oppression he had had to endure, his lack of support, his own mistakes, even. Nonetheless, she was persuaded that with his aptitudes, he could easily find a good job, at least a part-time one working for a mechanic or doing security, or even get a two-year degree in computer science and get himself a career. But there always seemed to be a reason not to cross a finish line of any sort, and that she did not understand.

However, she took great care to love her husband, as Ephesians 5 instructs, and support his endeavors, because she also wanted to see him succeed in whatever desires he had in his heart, like music, even if that meant that they would have to struggle financially for a time. She would be there for him, because she loved him and wanted him to be happy. When he was happy, he was fun to be around, and he could make the whole family laugh; he was humble and even made fun of himself. When Loammi was content, the family was at peace and the kids were happy. He would even stop worrying about everything for a while, and pray to God, and that made Marine feel safe.

SLOWLY, LOAMMI LEARNED TO rely on the fact that his wife could bear a lot of the family burdens without caving. Unlike him, who in spite of having talent and so many good qualities continued to struggle, she made things happen. In fact, everything Marine touched was bearing fruit, and that told him that God was truly with her. Every time bad news struck, she did not lose faith but persevered in her actions, and eventually things worked out. She had peace, and she had joy.

He remembered a time when he was stressed out because they were a month's rent behind. In all honesty, that was his fault. He had spent money he shouldn't have and could not make up for it. He did feel bad about it and had offered to pawn equipment to make up for the loss, but Marine had told him that it would not help in the end; it would be another debt.

So, she did what she did best. She took it to God, and God answered her.

"Honey, you have no idea how God has answered my prayer!" she yelled, running to him. "I told him 'Well, Lord, we've gotten behind, and I would truly need another paycheck to pay this month's rent. I can't mathematically make it. What can I do? How can you help me? You are my provider.' And I went just now to talk to the people at the office, and not only was the lady understanding, I felt like God was speaking to her heart; she told me not to worry about this month's rent! Is God amazing or what?"

Amazing, that's right, thought Loammi. There was that time when they did not have money for a new car after their old piece of junk finally gave out. He had been so depressed about that! But her? She just prayed. She didn't even worry about it. And then someone just gave her a car!

There was also the time when they had worried about an X-ray the doctor took that showed a deviation in her trachea, and she prayed with her church. Then on the next visit, that was gone! Even the doctor, with all her knowledge, had no word for that! A miracle, that's what it was.

While Marine's relationship with God was beautiful to watch unfold, Loammi found it also a bit irritating, at times, to see the way that God seemed to answer her prayers. After all, she wasn't all that, she wasn't perfect and holy, but God seemed to answer her every time. So, maybe she was just the blessing he was waiting for to finally win in this life.

"Baby, you are the best wife I could have wished for. You're like the lifeline between me and God. And we will win together. It's like God is saying, 'I won't pick up your calls, but you can put your wife on the phone.'"

So, Loammi committed to doing his best to love his wife. He knew the ways of the world, and he knew how easy it was to make women fall head over heels in love with him, because he was smooth, and his music was amazing; but he loved his wife and he wanted to please God. She had found favor in his eyes because she had clearly found favor in God's eyes. Nothing was new under the sun but the hand of God. Loammi knew that much. In the end, he wanted to win more than stardom in this life, receive the approval of God, and not lose his ticket to Heaven. He wanted to be on God's side.

But while he sought to be a good husband to her, Loammi expected his wife to be good to him also. Now that he had married her, she had become fully his, and according to the Bible, they were now one and the same. Loammi was the head, and his wife was the body. She owed him respect and obedience, and he had rights over her body. That was nothing he invented— that principle was clearly laid-out in the Word of God—and knowing this reinforced Loammi's assurance that he was in charge of her, as a king is a ruler over his land. Perhaps that was the reason why he felt entitled to those services that people who love you naturally provide, such as a meal, a conversation, or even a reassuring presence, at any time of the day or night.

"Babe?"

Loammi gently rocked Marine's shoulders. How can a woman half his size feel so heavy when laden with sleep? Her body did not move an inch and her eyes still did not open; the gentle movement of her nostrils opening and closing was the only sign that confirmed she was indeed alive. He sighed and looked at the ceiling through the dark of the night. How interesting that at 3:15 a.m., darkness suddenly revealed the shapes and hues of the things around you if you stared at them long enough. How could his wife sleep so peacefully? Loammi was tired too; he had worked on a tune and finalized all the sounds—an achievement, he thought—but he could not get to sleep. Thoughts were running through his head faster than he could keep them captive: What was he doing with his life? Why wasn't his career moving forward? What if he was not destined for success? What if failure was his sole footprint on this earth? That would explain why his mama left him at birth . . .

"Baby, wake up!"

"Hmmm . . . " Marine's body rolled over. Progress.

"Honey, wake up. I can't get to sleep."

"What . . . ?" Marine's face was now getting distorted. Her nose scrunched up and her mouth tightened to produce, as with effort, this one word. Then, her arm suddenly flew across her face. Loammi pulled it back gently.

"Love," he said, "I can't get to sleep. Can you rub my head? I have all these thoughts in my head and they won't let go. I need you."

"I'm sleeping!" she raged, rolling over on the mattress.

Loammi was surprised at the sudden change of appearance his previously peaceful wife was taking. The angel was now turning into a beast.

"How lovely that you are sleeping, princess; I want to get my beauty sleep too!" he said ironically.

Half-awake, Marine knew from habit that he would not leave her alone; besides, he had already disturbed her sleep.

"I have to wake up at six to go to work!" she whined.

"That's right," her husband replied, "I forgot you don't like to spend time with your man."

Marine sighed. She was tired and now disturbed. *What was wrong with him?* she thought. Perhaps it was true that their schedules were just off. He went to bed so late, and she worked all day. Why couldn't he play music during the day? Even when he laid down with her, he always got up during the night to go back to his keyboard. Did the man ever get a straight seven hours of sleep? she wondered.

"OK," she capitulated, "just give me a minute to wake up."

"Do you want coffee?"

"Sure," she replied.

Once she was fully awake, Marine enjoyed talking with her husband in the middle of the night just the two of them, when he was sober, and the rest of the world was asleep. During these moments, he was willing to share what was going on in his mind, and she felt drawn to him on a deeper level. But sleep interruptions were too abrupt and made it hard to function the next day, after not getting enough rest. She didn't understand how Loammi could keep a sane mind with such poor sleeping patterns. And if she truly thought about it, it was a selfish thing on his part to act this way toward her. It would not come to her mind to wake him up from his sleep unless there was an emergency. Why couldn't he think of other ways to spend quality time with her? Why was he so selfish in this way? Or needy? Why did he feel so entitled, and how could he discard even her basic need to sleep?

5

The Jealous Type

"For jealousy is the rage of a man: therefore he will not spare in the day of vengeance."

—PROV 6:34

KING SAUL'S CHARACTER HAD now become less admirable. Though he had lost God's approval, his heroic aptitudes as king of Israel continued to sustain his reputation, and his army went on to accumulate victories. Though Saul's fate was to be cut off from kingship, God's favor remained with Israel, so he continued to protect his cherished land and chosen people, albeit through King Saul. And the foreknowledge that David would someday take the throne set the scene for Saul's rising jealousy.

As Saul and his army returned triumphant from their long battle with the Philistines, they were greeted as conquerors by the people. News of their victory had been told in all of Israel, and many came to salute them with cheers and praise. The Word of God details that the women came out from all the cities of Israel to greet Saul's army with singing and dancing, tambourines and triangles, and screaming and cheering. They were singing to each other, saying how Saul had defeated thousands . . . and David, ten thousands!

David, who was now one of Saul's soldiers, had received attention. The remarkable story of this young man who had bravely fought a giant whom all feared had spread far and wide. His heroic fame now surpassed that of King Saul, and this reversal of fate displeased the incumbent king.

When he heard that David was acclaimed above him, Saul was infu-
riated, and jealousy started filling up his spirit. Perhaps he felt shame that
someone beneath his status and as small as David could be a better man of
war than himself. After all, Saul had conquered the heart of all of Israel ever
since he had been crowned king, and he was now losing footing to another, so
a seed of jealousy was planted in his heart, and it grew. Saul, who had loved
David for his excellence, was now starting to loathe him for the same reason.
Even though David was loyal to the king, he had become a threat to Saul. It
says that from that day forward, King Saul looked at David with a wicked eye,
as if he had become his enemy. (1 Sam 18:6–9)

IN THE FIRST FEW years of her marriage, Marine was satisfied with her
life, her husband and two children, her position, and her relationship with
God; her emotional needs were fully met. She did not have everything she
wanted, but she was content with what she did have. She was a cup-half-full
kind of girl. She loved her family, and their financial struggles seemed to be
coming to an end. Things were looking up. After more than eight years of
study, she was very close to finishing her doctorate and would be able to take
on a full-time job. It was about time one of them could adequately support
this family. Maybe Loammi would be less depressed once they had more
money and could put his mind into his music. It was disappointing to see
his talent waste away because of one thing or another. One of his friends and
also a neighbor, Mo, had acknowledged that Loammi had a unique talent
and suggested that he should market himself better. Mo had wanted to help
him, but Loammi—who always ended up suspicious of people—had not
taken his offer seriously. "God, please, open doors for him!" Marine prayed.

Doors opened indeed, but Loammi did not walk through them. Just
like the time when another neighbor had offered him a side job doing a
renovation, which would have been perfect part-time work for him! But
again, there seemed to always be an excuse, and Marine knew that even if
he tried, he wouldn't have followed through with it. Marine resisted resent-
ing him for that, because she knew that it was not that Loammi was a lazy
man; when he wanted to, he could work very hard, and he certainly wanted
to provide for his children. She came to believe that he lacked confidence
in himself. There was also another reason that she believed influenced his
rejection of that particular offer.

The neighbor, Chase, lived two doors down with his wife Sandra.
Sandra was a soft-spoken and discreet woman studying toward a master's
in biology. Marine regularly saw her walk to and from her car but seldom
had a chance to speak with her. In contrast, her husband Chase was quite a

chatterbox. Looking at his jovial demeanor and her kind temperament, one could see that Chase and Sandra were happy people. Marine knew that to be true, because she had joined them in church a couple of times with her son before she met Zsófia. At that time, she and Loammi had just started dating. Loammi had met Chase because he was often outside making small talk with Marine when Loammi arrived at her townhouse. One particular day, Loammi had texted Marine that he was on his way over. She was outside trying to set up a swimming pool for her then four-year-old son, as the temperature was close to ninety degrees. Chase walked by and started a conversation. Seeing her blowing into the plastic tube, he chuckled and offered to give her a hand.

"It's going to take you forever if you do it like that!" he had mocked. "I have a pump you can borrow if you want; I just need a minute to find it in my house."

Marine had followed him two doors down and entered through the doorstep of his townhouse. She waited in the entrance since the front door was wide open, and Chase retreated farther inside his house. Within five minutes, he returned, holding what looked like a tool a bit more sophisticated than a bicycle pump.

"Here," he said, "you can return it anytime."

Marine thanked him and walked out. Loammi was probably going to be there soon, and she was hoping to get the pool fully set up by then. Her son had invited a bunch of friends, and the boys were eagerly waiting in their bathing suits for the water to fill the pool. Thanks to Chase's generosity, that goal was accomplished in record time. Marine returned the pump to Chase. Then she went back and opened the back door of her own townhouse, which was unlocked, and was happily surprised to see Loammi inside. He was holding a small vase with a red rose in it but wore a frown on his face.

"Where were you?" he asked.

Marine explained that she had borrowed the neighbor's pump, and Loammi must have arrived while she was in his house. Loammi's face contorted and the frown intensified. A glare of light reflected from the sun into his eye, and for a second, Marine was blinded and could see only the shadow of a man while the interior of her home got dark. If he had not spoken at that moment, she may have wondered who that stranger was.

"You actually went inside his house?" he asked.

Marine was surprised that this bothered Loammi. Listening to his perspective, she could understand that perhaps walking into a man's house when his wife was not home could be misconstrued, but Chase and Sandra were not that type of people. Chase talked with everybody in the community, which was mostly made-up of women; he was practically one of the girls!. It just so happened that his wife had a different schedule and personality. If nothing else, Marine thought that Loammi should extend some trust to her since he knew her; she did not appreciate that he threw the rose he had brought into the garbage. Loammi made a big deal out of the incident and asked Marine to go to the neighbor's house later that evening and apologize to Sandra.

Marine felt that his suspicions were unreasonable and his request de-meaning; yet, she had been involved in an illicit relationship in the past and carried remnants of guilt from her youthful ways. This convinced her to accept Loammi's jealousy and judgement. It felt somewhat humiliating to apologize to a woman she barely knew and who probably wondered what hell she was trying to stir up in her household. Though Sandra was graceful and kind, Marine never forgot the awkwardness of the conversation.

WITH TIME, MARINE NOTICED that Loammi's reactions and fears had alienated some of their neighbors. Now that they were married, she knew him better, and as his wife, she sought to build him up and worked to keep her own faith from waning. She wanted to remain a strong wife who would truly stand by her man's side and honor the Lord. She believed that if she truly showed him the love of Christ, Loammi would be profoundly touched, as God promised in First Corinthians. Love is what would reach him, and in her mind there was nothing more extraordinary than seeing God change a man from bitter to grateful, from broken to whole. She could only imagine how wonderful it would be for her children to witness a man transformed by Jesus. Surely, they would be inspired forever, and God's glory would impact their family for years to come and perhaps even reach her own parents. Perhaps God could change Loammi, and perhaps he could also change her father.

Through all their troubles, Marine remained an optimist and was thankful to have friends to rely on. She still loved going to church on Satur-days. It was a safe place where God's presence reigned over every member of the congregation. She loved to hear her fellow Christian brothers and sisters give testimonials; she had given a few herself, and her faith had become very strong. Zsófia and her family had moved back to Hungary, and though she missed her friend's company, Marine found the same joy in going to church as before. Her children, too, enjoyed those evenings. The way her son prayed was humbling to her; at just seven years old, he had a pure faith and did not have to fight against his selfish nature as much as she did sometimes. She remembered how he had told them that he saw an angel in his bedroom.

It happened a few weeks ago, as he was lying in bed after dinner, waiting to fall asleep. He told his mom and dad in complete amazement that this angel, this being, was strong and blue. He was peaceful. He had huge thighs and arm muscles, and he came toward him and touched him. Marine and Loammi were in awe.

"Did he say anything to you?" Loammi asked.

The child answered, "No, he just touched me on the shoulder."

"You are so blessed, baby. This is amazing!" replied Marine, feeling goosebumps on her skin.

If it weren't for testimonials such as those that Marine heard around her on a continual basis, as well as many answered prayers, Marine would eventually have been swooped into the whirlwind of negativity that encompassed her husband, and her faith would have been weakened. But the evidence of God's presence and love around her allowed her to bear the moods, the anger, and the fits of drunkenness that Loammi filled their house with on a regular basis. Because she believed that he loved her and knew that he loved their children, Marine developed a mechanical response to make excuses for his character flaws, in spite of the fact that sometimes he took things too far.

With time, Marine realized that envy and jealousy were part of the problem that stopped her husband from completing any goal. He was in the habit of talking to the family for what seemed like hours, especially when he was drinking, and in those moments he often revealed his inner conflict about his failures as a musician:

"I am better than them all, you guys! I am better than Prince and them. I met them all by the way! You see, son, your dad could be out there right now with the Jay Zs and the Lil Waynes, and the whole world would bow down to my music. But see, I never wanted to sell my soul, and I will never bow down to the Devil. He can have the fame and everything. The Bible says, what is the point if a man gains the whole world but loses his soul? Huh? But know that your dad is the best of them all!"

Those types of drunken rantings were almost amusing, but they also saddened Marine's heart. At other times, things got more frightening.

One evening, Marine called Loammi after leaving the grocery store.

"Honey, would you like me to pick up some burgers on the way home? I don't feel like cooking. I'll be there soon."

There was a lot of traffic that day because of the unpredictable winter weather, so it took longer than expected for Marine to arrive home.

"I'm sorry, honey, there was a lot of traffic."

"Well, the kids are hungry!"

Loammi was mad. He started pacing back and forth. She hated when he did that, because it was typically the first sign that rage was to follow.

"Tell me, I'm just curious, what was at the store that it took you so long to get back to your family? Or rather, *who* was at the store?"

"No one was at the store; I don't like what you are you trying to suggest. There was a lot of traffic."

"But really, what, or who, attracted you that much at that store that you were willing to spend hours there, disregarding the fact that your husband and kids, even, were waiting for you? The kids were hungry."

"I said I was sorry; I left the store when I called you. I did nothing wrong. There was a lot of traffic and that's it." Then she could not help but correct him: "And it didn't take me hours, it took me forty-two minutes."

She had counted the minutes because she had learned to be precise in order to avoid being in the wrong. When he was upset, he was quick to accuse her, so she had to prepare a defense just in case. She set up the kids at the table and gave them their food. Loammi grabbed his burger. Without warning, he threw the burger at full speed against the wall. Squirts of ketchup and mustard were suddenly on the wall and in her hair.

"That burger is cold!"

Angry, embarrassed, and scared, Marine did not know what to say. The kids had frozen, and the atmosphere in the kitchen filled with tension. He walked away. The children hurried to eat so they could go to bed.

Loammi's jealousy ended up being one more negative thing she could expect from her husband. Somehow it would always flare up, and it was hard to calm him down because, most of the time, those feelings were completely unfounded. He had accused her before of staring at a man too intensely or spending too much time talking with a neighbor's husband. She read in the Bible that jealousy was cruel as the grave, and not an emotion to play with. She knew Loammi was wrong. She used to think about the tragedy of *Othello*. In the play, the prince is tricked into falsely accusing his wife, Desdemona, of having an affair and has her killed. It is only after she dies that he realizes his error, but it is too late. His unleashed jealousy had caused him to distrust the one he loved the most.

Even though Marine's troubles were on a smaller scale than those of Desdemona, she was very grieved to see her husband not listen to reason nor to God. To her, Loammi shared with the Moorish prince Othello a propensity to be led astray by strong and stubborn emotions. "How the flesh is deceptive indeed!" she would lament. Of course, that was a Shakespearian play and its ending made for good drama; Marine certainly did not wish nor anticipate anything like that to happen in real life. Not in this day and age,

THE JEALOUS TYPE   49

anyway. Besides, Loammi was not totally crazy with jealousy; he was just a bit paranoid at times.

However, to keep the peace, Marine learned what her husband liked, what he valued— such as loyalty and honor—and what bothered him. She sought to fix everything she could fix, and gave the rest to God in prayer. It became apparent that Loammi was more and more troubled by her going to church every week. Saturday services conflicted with him getting ready to go out and perform, meet other musicians, and go to the club—to net-work, as he called it. One day he made a sour remark that she took to heart, and though he had not said it openly, she understood that it would make him happier if she stopped going and instead spent that time focusing on his needs.

Loammi's jealousy had been the cause of several disputes. Oh, it was not always about the fact that she was late, or that she stared at a man a few seconds too long that caused him to be upset; sometimes Loammi was jeal-ous of the time she spent with her friends, or with the children, rather than with him. And yet other times it was the opposite: he would encourage her to see her friends, and focus on her happiness. That contradictory attitude made it difficult for Marine to anticipate which course of action to take, so she tried to avoid giving him any reason to arouse his jealousy. Because Loammi was starting to say bad things about her church, she came to the conclusion that she should attempt to put him first and give it up in order to win his heart for God and see this transformation she was so desperate for! God would still be with her through his Word.

Loammi never seemed to notice that she stopped going to church. He never asked about it and took for granted that his wife would spend her Sat-urday evenings at home, where she could give her affections to him. In spite of the sacrifice she had made—which appeared to have gone unnoticed— there was always something else to incite Loammi's heart to jealousy. At times, it even seemed that he was jealous of his wife's relationship with God.

"I gave you God!" he would rage, when they argued.

"You have no such power," she responded.

Marine hated arguing about God, but she hoped that her husband's jealousy would stir in his spirit a desire for Jesus himself, just like the Gen-tiles are said to be used by God to provoke Israel to jealousy, so that in the end they would return to Jesus. That was exactly what Marine wanted, and what God, in his Word, also said that he wanted. She was willing to make many more sacrifices to see that purpose fulfilled.

WHEN MARINE FINISHED HER doctoral degree, Loammi was very proud of her. He called her "Doctor" and "Professor," despite the fact that she had explained to him over and over that you are not a professor until you first become an assistant professor, then get a tenure track at a college or university. The road to a better financial footing because of her degree was paved with its own obstacles. It was almost like doing another dissertation: there were more dues to be paid. Deep inside, her desire to become a professor had diminished. It seemed like a lot of work, and she was weary. She had hoped that she could settle in a small college. She had set her hopes on two colleges in particular, and from the few interviews she had done, she was optimistic about her odds; but in the end, she was not hired. The rejection saddened her greatly. She ended up changing course slightly and found a temporary teaching position, until another opportunity offered itself in New York.

"Gosh, I don't know that I want to move to New York," said Loammi at first. "It is the Babylon of America, and God warns us to run from places like that."

Of all the Bible books, Loammi loved Revelation the most. He particularly enjoyed reading about the wrath of God being meted out to all the wicked doers; he felt a sense of justice and relief to know that oppression, racism, poverty, and other evils would not last forever.

Since it was Marine's only long-term option, she had to take the job. Loammi looked at the other side of the coin. He was a musician; maybe he could finally make it in New York. It was worth a try. For a couple of years at least, to see if they liked it. So, she went to the interview out east and got the job. He was excited to hear that.

"How do you feel, babe?"

"I'm overwhelmed," she said over the phone. "I'll tell you more about it when I get home."

Hours later, after she had taken a plane and a taxi, Marine looked forward to a good night's sleep in the arms of a happy husband. He had a lot of questions, and she chirped away, excited and proud of herself. But suddenly, when they got to talk about the salary that she had been offered, Loammi appeared quite disappointed.

"That's it?" he said. "It's not any better than what you'd get here! This is New York; you'd need three times, or at least two times the money. How are we going to survive there?"

He got silent. Not the peaceful kind of silent, but that same kind as when he would pace back and forth. And then the sound he made with his mouth, "mmm, mmm . . . " She despised that sound; it often foreshadowed that something bad was about to happen.

"You're worthless!" he finally uttered.

How dare you? How can you insult me when I am doing all the work? You should be ashamed of yourself! You're an awful man; I've never called you or your music worthless! I can't believe what you just said. You don't deserve me, and I wish I could slap you right now! Those were the thoughts that went through her head but never made their way out. Marine said nothing. Was it because she was angry? Scared?

In her bed, the words of Ephesians 4:26 danced before her eyes: "Let not the sun go down upon your wrath." Yes, Lord, she thought, but not tonight. I am angry; this man does not deserve anything!

In the morning, she tried to talk to her husband and let him know how unfair he had been to speak to her like that. She reminded him how hard she worked, and that he really needed to get a job himself—then she would not have to work as hard!

He apologized. He said he was afraid of moving to New York, but he was hopeful that good things would happen; he would do everything he could to make opportunities open there and to support his family.

"I love you, baby. All I want is to be able to make it so I can take care of you guys."

"Yeah, I know."

While "sorry" was a word Loammi used a lot, Marine wondered if it had become a mantra to avoid introspection; he seemed to have delusions that things came easy to everyone but him, and he both envied and resented that. She knew something was wrong with him—perhaps low self-esteem? Because of his emotions and reactions, she was resigned to keeping some feelings shut in so as to avoid starting up trouble. Whatever that disease was that aroused jealousy and paranoia in him, Marine had a feeling it would not go away.

6

The Angry Man

"He that is slow to anger is better than the mighty; and he that ruleth his spirit than he that taketh a city."

—Prov 16:32

Once jealousy had taken root in Saul's heart, the king became an angry man. Anger controlled his attitude toward his servant David, leading to the first incident of Saul's abusive behavior: one day, the evil spirit of the Lord took hold of Saul and moved him in a trance throughout his house. David grabbed his harp and started playing, as he usually did when Saul fell ill. But this time, instead of being appeased by the music, Saul grabbed his spear and attempted to pin David against the wall.

David was able to duck the blow twice. Little information is provided in the Word of God about his emotional reaction, but we can infer that he must have been quite shocked to see the king that he respected, served, and loved, attempt to do him harm.

Saul continued to be angry with David. He started plotting against him. He put David in charge of a thousand men and sent him into battle to put him in harm's way. Luckily for David, God's protection was over him, and he won every battle he fought, not to mention the respect of the people of Israel.

David's continual victories caused Saul's anger to grow into an obsession to bring his servant down. Because David was so popular with the people, however, Saul did not want to kill him publicly—instead, he devised a scheme to lead him to death. In a sense, Saul was acting like an abusive man does: he continued to hurt his companion, but he had enough sense to not do it in front of others. Saul promised David the hand of his eldest daughter, Merab, if he proved his loyalty in battle. Saul was, one more time, setting the scene to have David fall in battle at the hands of the Philistines. David, pure of heart, was touched by the honor bestowed upon him and felt a duty to serve his king. But when the time came for him to claim the hand of Merab, Saul had given her to another man to marry.

Saul's deception was similar to the psychological manipulation abused partners undergo. Often, the "victim" ends up second-guessing him or herself. It sounds like David, much like an abused victim, justified the behavior of his abuser. He told Saul's servants that he was not fit to be the king's son-in-law, for he was, after all, a servant of low descent.

Like an abuser, Saul was studying others. He used information he learned from his servicemen—that David felt unworthy of the king's honor, and that his daughter Michal was enamored of David—to trick his servant once more. This time, Saul offered David the hand of his daughter Michal if, in lieu of a dowry, David defeated and brought him the foreskins of one hundred Philistines.

Saul was using manipulative tactics because jealousy had turned him into an angry man, and anger causes a man to do wrong rather than to seek wisdom. It says that Saul's anger was the result of his fear; he could see that David was good and favored by God, and that he himself was losing control of his kingdom. Saul wanted the publicly adored David to fall at the hands of Israel's enemies, so he would regain control of his kingdom, and of himself; he wanted to be whom he had been when he was a charmer.

David accepted Saul's offer and went to battle, defeated the enemy, and brought back their foreskins as the king had requested. This time, Saul had no choice but to give him his daughter Michal in marriage. Seeing that his daughter loved David and that God favored him, Saul's purpose to kill his servant became an obsession. David started to fear King Saul, who he came to know as an enemy all his life.

Often, children of an abusive parent end up carrying the unfair weight of being the peacemakers—appeasing the villain and protecting the victim. Jonathan, the son of Saul, knew about his father's anger and his attempted assault on David. He tried to intervene on David's behalf, and made his father, the king, swear before God that he would not put his hands on David again. With Jonathan looking out for him, David was able to resume his life at the palace, in Saul's presence.

But eventually, the wicked spirit that was in Saul took hold of him again, and another assault took place. While David played the harp, Saul tried to *pierce him with his spear again! David ran for his life into the night and took refuge by the prophet Samuel's home, near Ramah—running to him as a victim pursued by an assailant runs to the police for safety. Saul sent a group of his men after David, but God took hold of them and poured his spirit on them so that they prophesied. By doing so, God got them all on David's side. Finally, Saul took it upon himself to go and search for David. But the spirit of God overtook him also; Saul prophesied and turned around. He rent his clothes and lay naked on the floor, surrendering to the power of God. (1 Sam 18:10—19)*

ON A BEAUTIFUL SUMMER day, the family was all packed up to make the big move to New York. Loammi would drive the rental truck and Marine the family car; he would take their son and she their daughter, and they would take turns following each other. For some reason, every time the family took a road trip, all was well. Perhaps it was the hope for a fresh start, the excitement of discovering a new life, or simply the sensation of freedom that North American freeways provide; at any rate, road trips were a bonding experience for the couple. They stopped to let the kids take a break from the boredom of sitting idle in a car, to use the bathroom, to fill up the tank, or to get a bite to eat. No complaints.

"What's going on, honey?" Loammi asked through the walkie-talkie they used to communicate between vehicles. "Are you girls OK? I see wild movements in the car; is everything OK?"

"Oh, yes, we just have a bee situation, and you know how she is around bees."

"Ah, that's what's going on. Do you want to exit at the next stop, honey?"

It was a long trip and a lot of work, but Marine enjoyed every moment of it. These were the times when Loammi acted as a protector, a reliable husband and father who could fix the car if it broke down, and make sure his family arrived safe and sound at their destination. It was a pleasant couple of days.

They settled in New York. There was excitement, there were places to discover, and adventures to have. Wealthy suburbs clashed with dirty and crowded cities, delineated by infrastructure wearing the rust of time. The road to the Big Apple, frequently under construction, gave way to noise and life.

Visiting the Big Apple was a treat for everyone. Loammi made those trips more often than the rest of the family, when he was looking for opportunities to network as a musician. The fact that everything was new gave him a false sense of expectation, as if suddenly the sky was wide open, and he could do anything without fear of failure.

Aside from visiting New York City, their favorite activity was to take a trip to Sandy Hook beach in New Jersey, a couple hours away from where they lived. Since it was still summertime and school hadn't started yet, they tried to enjoy the beach as often as possible. With swimming suits, towels, toys, snacks, and a few beers in the trunk, they were on their way. Nothing was better than the caress of the wind on the beach boardwalk and the purifying touch of the ocean! Loammi, who had never been to the ocean before, fell in love. It was beautiful, it was natural, it was new.

For a while, life in New York offered many promises. They befriended neighbors, the parents of their children's closest classmates, and other delightful persons with whom they associated. They particularly enjoyed spending time with a Christian couple, Dave and Diana, who lived in Montclair, New Jersey. Marine enjoyed the school where she started teaching, the kids had a lot of friends, and everyone was happy and successful. Everyone, that is, except for Loammi.

Somehow, it became more difficult than he had imagined to carve opportunities for himself to be a musician. He told himself, as one recites a mantra, that they really didn't have enough money to allow him to go to New York often enough, and so he was not able to get sufficient exposure and opportunities as a musician. They lived far from the City in a neighborhood that, though relatively safe, was still much less safe than back home in the Midwest. On top of not having enough money, Loammi believed that he didn't have the time to commute every day to New York City, because he had to be at the bus stop when his children got out of school, since Marine worked school hours every day as a teacher, and since there was no way that he could leave them by themselves. The more time went by, the more he realized that it would take a lot more than he thought to make it in this big city, and he would have to be extremely lucky. This realization slowly eroded the hopes he had felt at first. He started spending more time at home, falling back into his old ways of making music rather than goals. He became more negative.

Marine started to believe that her husband had accepted failure as the norm. She desperately wanted to see him happy and made an effort to support his endeavors. She was happiest when he was in good spirits and feeling optimistic. She helped him edit his album cover, find the right font, and clean up his descriptions. Then one day, he finally took the bull by the horns and registered to go sing at the Apollo, the famous theater where many successful musicians got their start. What an exciting time for everyone: Dad was going to do something great! Except that he started to get cold feet, and the night before, he considered not going.

Marine prayed hard that night; for the first time she thought about what it would be like to leave Loammi. Suddenly she looked back over their life together and wondered if she had played a part in his failures—if she was enabling him to remain stuck in his ways. She had been very excited for her husband, but he was letting himself and his family down again, and she wanted to understand why. She had worked hard to be a good wife and make a home for her children; what more did God want from her? Why would God have given her a husband who led her to Christ, but she in return produced no fruit in her husband's life? Was she inadequate as a Christian? This time instead of internalizing Loammi's pain, she looked at his failures objectively, and begged God to intervene. By the morning, God—being a prayer-answering God—had calmed her husband's spirit and returned him to reason.

Loammi performed to the Apollo and was extremely well received by the crowd, as he usually was during his gigs back in the Midwest. Everybody loved him and cheered for his talent. Feeling on top of the world, he took the whole family out to eat! For weeks his successful appearance at the Apollo was his conversation starter with all musicians he met and his sole preoccupation. He had accomplished a goal and it focused all his energy; suddenly, his happiness revolved around it. He reminisced over how the crowd had cheered for him and how he had so much to do to prepare for the next competition! He was determined to not let his fans down, nor himself.

Unfortunately, he did not win in the next competition, and so the road down Apollo lane stopped there. Marine worried that Loammi would not persist and would fall back into the negativity he had displayed in the last few years. Indeed, he slowly sank back into his dark moods and his drinking. There was a particular whiskey that seemed to have a very negative effect on him, more so than any other liquor he ever drank. Marine hated when he bought it, because he turned into a wicked nightmare. One Saturday afternoon, as they were watching a movie, he started sipping that whiskey. At first, they lounged cozily in the couch. The movie was about lawyers who were making pacts with the Devil—Marine's most dreaded kind of movie, but her husband's most fascinating. When watching what she thought of as a bad movie, Marine was in the habit of anticipating how her husband was going to analyze it. Certainly, her scholarly training had prepared her for these systematic observations, but what she was really trying to do was brace herself for Loammi's reaction. When the screen displayed a scene where the female character cheated on her husband and had erotic encounters with demons, Marine started to worry.

At the end of the movie, Loammi was thinking. He was quiet but not at rest. Then, he started to talk. He said that all women are evil in their make-up and that God named Adam's wife Eve, from the word "evil," to make it clear that evil comes from women. As he spoke, he became more passionate. It spiraled downward and Loammi's anger was now directed at Marine; all of a sudden, he slapped her across the face. Shocked, hurt, and angry, Marine instantly yelled at him, then ran away. He ran after her, caught up with her, and pushed her against the wall with both hands around her neck. Panicked, she could not breathe. She had never been in such a powerless situation, and fear flowed through her veins.

"I'm sorry, I'm sorry; please, I beg you, stop!"

"Dad, let her go!"

The kids had run into the room after their parents and were screaming. Loammi let go.

The shock. The humiliation. The awkwardness. Marine did not know how to process what had happened. She stood frozen in her body and in time. She could not think rationally. Why and how did this happen? Did her husband really grab her by the neck? She thought of running away. In her mind, she could see herself become a strong woman and march into the living room where Loammi had settled back in, take her children by the hands, and raise her voice with confidence: Who do you think you are? How dare you attack me? I'm taking my kids! Goodbye, you monster! But in reality, as she looked around, she felt trapped. How could she leave the house? He was now predictably wicked and had waged war. Perhaps for the first time, Marine was actually scared of him, and the fear paralyzed her. If she attempted to run and take the children, Loammi would certainly not let that happen; how would they get through the door? Her thoughts and her heart were racing, trapped in a space and time that had projected her outside of her normal reality, and she did not know what to do with that.

As time inched forward, it appeared that peace had settled back in, but Marine knew that she wanted to get out. She tried to wish away what had happened and took refuge in the bathroom, where the mirrors reflected their side of the story, and she saw the blue marks around her neck. She did not want to believe it, but she could not close her eyes to reality.

She walked into the living room. Everyone was quiet. Loammi was on the phone with his sister. He was acting like himself again—his *good* self. Her children were playing a video game. Marine knew that this was an opportunity. She said that she was going to get some groceries for dinner, before it got dark, and would be right back.

"OK, honey, I love you," Loammi uttered, before resuming his phone conversation. "Sis says 'hi!'"

"OK, say 'hi' to her back," Marine said as calmly as possible.

She opened the door handle and got out. Fresh air! Freedom! Quickly, she got into her car. Suddenly her body started to shake. Her hands had a hard time fastening the seat belt, and her right leg trembled uncontrollably, which made it hard to make good contact with the pedals. She had to tell someone what happened. She called a friend back home in the upper Midwest.

"I don't know what to do!"

"Do you think the children are safe with him?"

"He's never hurt the kids."

"Go to the police."

"I'm afraid of going to the police. I don't want him to go to jail."

"Then go to the hospital. You need help for yourself. They will help you and make sure you're OK."

Marine liked that idea. She would not have to send Loammi to jail, and she did have trouble thinking rationally—maybe she was going crazy? Going to the hospital seemed like the right thing to do. Once there, she disclosed what happened and they dispatched a police officer.

The officer explained to Marine that in the state of New York, domestic assault is a very serious crime and punishable by law. She exhaled. She was not crazy; it was him. It was Loammi who had done wrong. Just like that, she felt safe—in this space, in front of these men in uniform with weapons by their sides, surrounded by nurses and doctors. She felt safe in this space where no one was threatening or yelling. She told them her children were with him, and that they had always been safe with their dad, but to make sure to bring them to her.

When the police arrested Loammi, he could not believe it. He had been looking for his wife all evening and was afraid that something had happened to her. He had recognized that he might have acted harshly toward her, and perhaps she was feeling bad. Maybe she had cried while driving and, because women are emotional—especially white women—she had been unable to get a hold of herself and crashed the car. Looking up at the dusk and then down at his unanswered texts and calls, Loammi started fearing the worst: maybe his wife had had an accident. When he saw those red and blue lights flashing outside, he ran out of the house to meet the police escort, fearing they had bad news to report. He was almost in tears. Then, the gripping anguish turned to shock as a man in uniform grabbed his hands, pulled them behind his back, and locked them with handcuffs. He was arrested. What? His wife, whom he felt sorry for, was doing this against him?

A WEEK HAD PASSED and Loammi, unsuccessful at finding someone to help him make bail, was still in jail. He was calling home every day, and spent hours on the phone, speaking with a lot of people. Marine had been going to church with their friends, Dave and Diana, from New Jersey. If Loammi had not called everyone they knew, she would not have told a soul. But he involved their friends and family, so she received their help. Dave visited Loammi in jail. Later over the phone, Dave gave his report as a man of God:

"Well, if I were you, I would be wary of your husband. As a pastor, I was able to go with him into a room and talk to him directly across a table. I tell you, Marine, I sensed a lot of tension in his entire body. At one point I felt that if there had not been a guard there, he would have probably punched me if he could. You see, there is a lot of anger in him; he has what is called 'worldly sorrow.' The Bible explains the difference between repentance—which is called godly sorrow—and fake repentance, which is worldly sorrow. That means that as he says he is sorry, what he is most sorry about is that he is sitting in jail, not that he hurt you, and by extension, his children. I would not believe him right now."

It took a few more weeks and a lot of prayers from Marine, Dave, and Diana until Loammi started showing signs of true remorse. Diana was a strong woman of faith, and Marine treasured her friendship. She trusted her.

"I will fast with you," offered Diana, "and pray, until God takes away the root of anger from Loammi's heart. I agree with you; I believe he is a good man, but he has a lot of anger, and unfortunately he does not see how it affects others."

Diana's wisdom encouraged Marine. The fact that her friends knew the difficulty she faced made a huge difference for her. She felt stronger. She felt that now she had people who would watch over her, protect her, and hold Loammi accountable when he returned home.

He had written several apologetic letters and had promised his children before God and in writing that he would never hurt their mama again. Stranded in New York, the family needed a return to normalcy, so, when they finally called Marine to prepare her for the trial, she did not go and the case was dismissed. Loammi came back home, and life returned to normal.

Until one night when Loammi came back from the liquor store with that same bad whiskey again . . . Marine started fearing again what would happen now that she knew what he was capable of. And worst of all, dusk was falling, and at nighttime the whole world is asleep, and there is no one to run to. This time, though, she would not wait for another assault. She started thinking of ways to create a safety plan with one goal: get out of here, but this time with the kids. Unfortunately, Loammi had her shut in the bedroom with him, and his ranting started to sound menacing.

"What?"

One of the children had knocked on the bedroom door. It was their son.

"I just want to make sure you guys are all right."

"It's OK, buddy. Mom and I are just talking; we're fine. Go and play."

Marine wondered how hard it must have been for her son to go back to his room and "play." He and her daughter were probably both terrified at that moment, as was she. She prayed that God would distract them, while she tried to reason with the beast. Loammi picked up the liquor bottle.

"Here, do you want some? Why not? Would you rather have a glass of wine?"

"Yes, thanks."

"Oh, you must be ready to die if you want a drink."

Terrifying as those words sounded to her ears, it was true that alcohol seemed appealing to Marine at that moment. It might take a bit of the fear away, and it would help her stop shaking.

"Do you realize how you betrayed your husband? Your king, even? I am your king, and you are my queen. But baby, you listened to that man while I was rotting in jail, in the filthiest jail in the world, in New York, even! You gave that man authority over my family, and you went onto his turf in his church. God knows what crazy things they do in that church! Do you know that priests rape little boys, even? Huh? Are you aware of that? And yet, you see me, your husband, as a dangerous man, and so you give the enemy a free pass!"

He paced back and forth in the room, taking another gulp straight from the bottle.

"What about the police, huh? Don't you know that every day those white police officers kill people with my skin color? But nowhere in your selfish little mind did it come to you that one of them could do that to your husband, huh? You were so self-centered and worried about your little self, when we just had a bad fight, that you were willing to bet my life on a game of Russian roulette! If instead of going to the hospital you had just come back home as a wife should, anyway, we would have just talked it out."

He walked toward her, and she jumped back. He grabbed her gently by the neck, and she gasped. He released his grip.

"Hey, chill out, baby; I'm not out to kill you. In fact, I've just proven to you that there is no way in hell I can kill my wife! I love you, baby."

He walked away, then turned back.

"But, if you ever do it again, if you ever try to turn against me again, to another man, or to the police, I will kill you!"

Standing tall and still, he took another sip of whiskey.

"I will cut you up in pieces and make sure you're dead this time!"

Panicked, Marine prayed silently: "Father, please give me a way out and I *promise* you that I will seize it!"

Her son knocked on the door again. How quickly God answered her prayers! What a great God!

"OK, little dude, we're finished here. Are you hungry? Do you want to go get something to eat? Go get your sister!

"Here, baby," he said to Marine, "you drive, 'cause I've been drinking."

It was about half past eight in the evening. The contrast between the peaceful night outside of the house and the terror she just experienced inside struck Marine as unreal. How could one moment feel like a time spent in hell, and the next minute her eyes witnessed the still of the evening? In the car, Loammi had calmed down, and the kids were quiet. Yet the only thing that Marine could think of was that she did not want to go back to that house with that man who may go back to his whiskey for the night. She also remembered the promise she made God, and so she had to get away from the beast he turned into, if only for the night.

When she arrived at the mall, she suggested that she and her daughter go get food while the men looked around at the shops, so the four separated. Marine was shaking. Now physically away from Loammi, a sensation of freedom overwhelmed her, and the fear of seeing him return gripped her as tightly as her little girl's hand in hers. She ran across a police officer, who listened to her account of the evening and took her to a room where other police officers were. She had no idea malls had police rooms. They arrested Loammi, and she was taken to the police station. There she was again, away from the threatening face of the monster that had jumped out of Loammi, sitting and staring at a piece of paper where she had to describe the incident that had happened to justify the arrest. Now feeling safe, Marine felt a bit of remorse when she wrote down what had happened on the police report.

The charges read, "Terroristic threat."

"Sign your name here, please."

The officer looked at her strangely, and for a moment she wondered if she was wrong to accuse her husband. Though she felt bad being at the police station with her children, she also felt good. She knew that they could go home safely. But her son was angry.

"I don't understand, Mom; what did Dad do this time? He was talking to me when you guys were in the mall, and he said how sorry he felt for ever hurting you that one time. We were waiting for you to bring back food. Why did you call the police this time? He didn't do anything!"

Marine felt even worse. She tried to explain to him that his dad had started drinking and she had not felt safe, and if you don't feel safe you call the police. Deep inside, she felt awful. Would it have been better if she had waited? Would Loammi have been able to contain himself and go to sleep if they had gone back home after the mall? Or would he have started drinking again? The worst part to her was that she had had to set him up while he was with their son. She had been instructed by the officers to call him on his cell phone, and pretend that they, the girls, had been in the bathroom, that they were picking up the food they ordered, and next they were going to meet them at the car.

"Are you at the car, honey? We're meeting you in just a few minutes."

Loammi waited for his wife and daughter, with his son, both of them hungry. But instead, the police flashed their lights at Loammi, and hand-cuffed him again. She felt sick.

"Well, it's unfortunate that you had to set him up," said Diana over the phone. "But Loammi needs to know that he inspires fear when he is angry, and he is going to have to deal with being in jail again."

Marine found solace in talking with the few friends and family members who knew about the situation. Loammi's uncle, Jim, was very sad to hear about this recidivism.

"I don't know what to do, Jim. I love him, but he needs help. One day, I remember, he was mad and threw the hamburger against the wall because it was cold and he said it took me too long to get home."

"Well, then you know that this is an unfair man. I love Loammi too, and I feel guilty because I wasn't there for him when he was little, and there were a lot of bad things going on. I often think I should have been there more. But I would love to see him happy."

"Yes, that's just it, he's just not happy with himself."

"Well, let him sit in jail. Honestly, I was talking to our cousin Babette and she said, 'Marine should just stop worrying about Loammi and go live her life!'"

Days later, Marine dwelt over those words as she was walking along Fifth Avenue in downtown New York, alongside Central Park; she felt the air flow through her hair while birds chirped in the trees in broad daylight, and suddenly she felt light as a feather.

This time, Marine did not take Loammi's phone calls for a while. He sat in jail, alone again, back in that same dirty hellhole he had just come out of. And he was angry—so much so that he got into a fight with a cellmate, and spent two days in solitary confinement.

7

The Promise-Breaker

"A double-minded man is unstable in all his ways."

—Jas 1:8

Jonathan met David in *Naioth, near Ramah. David cried out to him: "What did I ever do to anger your father?" David wanted to make sense of Saul's vendetta against him. David had been loyal to Saul, but it was clear that the king wanted him dead. Confused, he still looked upon Saul with a pure heart and as the anointed king chosen by God; he persisted to see good in him. He assumed that Saul had hidden this personal feud from Jonathan so as not to hurt his son's feelings, since he knew that David and Jonathan had a deep friendship. Jonathan also tried to see goodness in his father. Saul had promised his son that he would not kill David, so Jonathan wanted to believe in that promise. Jonathan agreed with his friend that whatever was wrong with the king, the great and eternal God could help him.*

Jonathan loved his father, and he wanted God to bless him. He also loved David like his own brother. One could say that Jonathan was caught in the middle of an abusive relationship, pulled between the two people he loved. Like David, Jonathan did not understand the sickness in Saul's spirit; he was confused about Saul's unstable and irrational ways. Could an intervention bring reconciliation? Could God persuade Saul to change his mind toward David? After all, Saul was the King of Israel, and like other spiritual men who came before him, Saul had a relationship with God! The honor and the loyalty that

63

both Jonathan and David had for Saul was genuine; they did not seek the anni-
hilation of Saul but the prosperity of his kingdom. As loved ones genuinely seek
the rehabilitation of a father figure, David and Jonathan considered what could
be seen as a back-in-the-day intervention to help the king return to the just and
loving ruler that he once was. They could tell that his behavior was not normal.

"What would you have me do?" asked Jonathan of David. Being the son
of the king, he had influence and was going to use it, just as children do when
they attempt to break up a fight between their parents. They plotted that Da-
vid would hide for three days, and if Saul got angry about his absence, they
would know that Saul was truly after David's life, and David would have to
leave the palace for good. But if Saul was not angered by David's absence, the
men would know that it was safe for David to come back to Saul's court. David
and Jonathan parted ways after praying to the Almighty God that he would
keep their household together. They promised eternal love and loyalty to each
other and between their houses, and David went away to hide and wait for his
friend to come back and let him know Saul's reaction.

When Saul noticed David's absence at the table and asked Jonathan
about it, his anger was greatly kindled. Jonathan must have been devastated as
he realized that all hopes for reconciliation were gone, and he could no longer
deny the danger that Saul posed to David, because Saul, the king, showed
himself to be a promise-breaker; he went against his word. Back then, words
spoken—especially by someone in a position of authority, such as a king—were
as binding as a signed contract would be in our day and age. Because the king
broke his word and Jonathan knew that David was truly in danger, he went to
warn his friend and say goodbye. Before they went their separate ways, David
and Jonathan promised that they would do whatever it would take to keep
the peace between their respective houses, and not harm the other. (1 Sam 20)

THIS TIME, IT TOOK effort on Loammi's part to make his way back home.
Unable to depend on Marine, he was alone with his thoughts. A man in a
cell has a lot of time on his hands to read the Bible and a lot of opportunities
to face his demons. In jail, God becomes the one true friend you have left.
Before long, Loammi was quoting Scripture in letters to his family. He saw
that everyone took his wife's side, even his own relatives; they expected him
to be accountable for his anger and drunkenness, for the wickedness that
came over him in the times that he had lost control of himself. During his
incarceration, he poured his heart out to God; he cried, and he made himself vulnerable. He let himself wallow in his heartache. He allowed others to
see his shame. This was not what he wanted his life to be; he truly wanted to
become a better version of himself.

Isolated in New York, and far from her own family and her in-laws, Marine was once again faced with the decision of giving her husband another chance, or leaving him. "Should I stay or should I go?" That was the most debated question in self-help books and talk shows about domestic abuse. The possibility of recidivism was real. If Loammi did not mean what he said, he could go back to being dangerous. Having to weigh the true intentions of a man is a heavy task, especially when you want to believe him. Probabilities are too objective to speak to your personal situation. Anything is possible, and your gut feeling can waver just as much as your emotions. The truth is that Marine was confused. On the one hand, Loammi was her husband and the father of her children. They had been together a long time, and he was her home. Marine knew him at his best. But she had also seen the worst of him, and those two sides were opposite forces.

She knew in her heart that the evil that tormented Loammi was not the core of the husband who loved his family and loved God. Marine knew that the real enemy was not her husband—that the wickedness in him was not the real Loammi—but a disease, an evil spirit to cast out, a thorn to remove. A wound to heal. A woman, whether she has children or not, often has a maternal instinct, even toward her husband. Marine could not forget about his wounded heart that cried out, during the drinking and in those beautiful songs, how it was robbed of maternal love.

When the time came to prepare for trial, Marine could not get herself to accuse her husband before a jury, and so the case was dismissed. In a sense, she felt like the choice was made for her, and like a die that had been cast, she let be what would be; that gave her a sense of relief, because deep down, she was not ready to make such a choice and accept full responsibility for its outcome. Maybe she was a coward at heart, or maybe she just had too much hope. Maybe she was indeed living in la-la land and approached Scripture the same way; or maybe she was selfish and dependent on someone to love her. Perhaps she looked at things the wrong way and did not know how to set proper boundaries in her life. Her children had wounds too, and needed to live in a loving and healthy environment. They needed peace, hope, and joy. But what better way to see the love of Christ and the power of God than in the restoration of their family unit? By that time, she had built a strong support system. Everyone they were close to was in the know: his friends, her friends, their families, and even the downstairs neighbors. Why couldn't victory be theirs?

Though Marine had doubts, she had put herself in a position to not give up. Faith, by definition, requires turning a blind eye to doubt. She knew that as Loammi's wife, she was qualified and had the duty to petition God for his restoration. While reason reminded her that there was a risk in letting him come back home, her heart wanted to believe that Loammi was touched by the Holy Spirit and God was opening his eyes; she could not leave and accept defeat for his soul.

"I gave my life to Jesus all over again, baby," he had said over the phone.

Love never fails, reads First Corinthians 13. What is the Word of God if love *does* fail?

LOAMMI'S UNCLE'S HEALTH WAS deteriorating, so the family decided to move back home to the upper Midwest at the end of the school year. They had lived peacefully during the last few months, and while they had enjoyed the hidden beauty of New York—both city and state—they were not unhappy about the upcoming move. The bad things that had happened on the East Coast haunted them like a ghost in the night.

As they packed everything and cleaned the empty house, the couple experienced a sense of inner cleansing. They were working together. And as surely as the trip to New York had filled them with the hopes of a new and bright future, so did the trip back home. It felt like a new anointing.

They were going to live with Loammi's sister and her husband. That arrangement was perfect, for in truth, Marine had never fully let go of the memories of fear; it was a relief to know that they would not be isolated but would have the support of relatives. She also appreciated the opportunity to get to know her sister-in-law better, and the children would have a bigger family. With aunts and uncles and cousins passing through, it was a house full of people and full of life.

For three months they all lived peacefully. Marine had gotten a new job, in an office this time. She enjoyed her new routine, with no homework to bring home. What a luxury! Loammi worked around the house while looking for a job, getting close to his brother-in-law, who made him want to be a better man. At first Loammi had told Marine that he understood why she had resorted to involving the police; he said he knew that she had no other choice and understood that his anger was the cause of her fears. He took responsibility for hurting her and his children. But slowly, his mindset changed, and the empathy he had extended to his wife, he now directed toward himself; in that process, the shame and contrition he had felt inside diminished as he turned the tables on her. It was not clear what caused this shift, but soon enough, something in his mind pushed him to believe that he was the one who had been wronged in that whole situation.

"You know," he said one day as they were alone in their car, "I've been wondering. What took you so long to get me out of jail? When it comes down to it, your love ain't that deep. You go with other people in a church where I didn't want you to go; you listen to the authority of another man rather than your own husband. You turn to the police, against me! You are not on my side. You're just like the world, just like every other white woman."

Marine was tired of the familiar yet awkward change of perspective that overcame her husband at any given moment. She also resented him when he brought up race in the argument because it felt punitive and divisive. It was as if he had cast her out onto the wrong side, making her feel guilty for the racially motivated police brutality that permeated life as Loammi knew it. From his perspective, she had sided with the enemy.

"I just want to ask you something," he continued. "I mean, you knew how horrible a place it was in jail and how hurt I was, and yet it seems that you were getting very comfortable letting me rot in a place like that. Really, you were getting quite comfortable, weren't you?"

Marine drove through the alleys that led to their in-laws with a weight on her shoulders. Her spirit sank in her heart as she pulled up to the house that was supposed to be their fresh start. Really, are we going down that green road again? she thought. The memories of her sleepless nights—of countless prayers, fasting, crying, keeping up a professional facade at work while her heart was broken—flashed through her mind.

"I just can't believe that you let me rot in that jail for so long! No wife that loves her husband does that! The only thing that makes sense is it must have been convenient for you. Tell me, who were you messing with? What man was keeping you from taking your husband back home—your king— where he belongs, with his queen?"

As Marine registered Loammi's accusations, she thought of the time that she had opted out of the end-of-semester faculty dance at school. She had signed up for the dance to get her mind off of her problems. But when she realized that that year, the faculty was paired with a member of the opposite sex, she had opted out, because she did not want to go to dance practice with a male colleague while her husband was in jail. She felt it would be disrespectful toward him because he did not know about it.

"I'm sure you let me rot in jail to hook up with somebody."

How could her husband be so far from the truth? And how could she prove him wrong?

"Yes, that's the only explanation that makes sense," he added. "How else do you explain not getting me home sooner? I had told you I was sorry; I had apologized. You knew I was sorry, and yet you still chose to keep me in that jail. That's not what love looks like! What was really going on?"

Loammi's words started making Marine doubt herself. She loved her husband. Should she have conquered her fears sooner? She knew she had not betrayed him with another man, but was her love weak? Had she failed to be the perfect wife God called her to be? She did remember feeling joy when she realized that she could talk to whomever she wanted to and say whatever she wanted to. She remembered the few moments when she actually felt freer without him. And now, here they were, sitting in a car and arguing over the same nonsense again.

She wanted to tell him that she was scared. It had taken years for her to become afraid of his unruly and violent spirit, and once he had crossed that line, fear had come into play. Was she at fault in any way to let fear in? Had she not realized his repentance when he offered it? But no! He was the one who acted unfaithfully, with violence and treachery! He was the one who turned into a dangerous maniac. He had to see that! His thinking did not make sense.

Marine wanted to defend herself. What an injustice on his part to accuse her of being unfaithful, when she had gone to hell and back because of him! What kind of vicious and stubborn mind game was this? She wanted to force him into *her* shoes for once and make him face a real-life monster—not the kind he faced in video games, but the kind that would make him lose control of his bowels.

"You don't know how scary you can get!" she pleaded.

It seemed to be an unfair twist of fate, but there was Loammi, accusing her of being unfaithful, and she could not prove her innocence with irrefutable evidence. This argument was setting both of them up for failure, as if orchestrated by outside forces playing them against each other, as on a chessboard. As one tries in vain to reason with the Devil, Marine's poor attempt at defending herself was countered on every side with the swiftness of a mind brighter than hers. As in a game of chess, when the queen is cornered, the king falls. Checkmate. But in this real-life game, neither of them won. Loammi would not hear her side of the story. Composed, he took off his wedding ring and put it away in his pocket. He opened the door to get out of the car and said:

"That's OK. I'll do the same."

Feeling angry and unjustly accused, Marine watched Loammi greet his brother-in-law with a big smile on his face, as if all were well. She started thinking about Othello again. You will be sorry, she lamented. God will show you how wrong you are, for everything, and you will be sorry!

Later that day, Loammi's family had planned a festive lunch. By the time the guests arrived, Loammi had put his ring back on. He seemed to be back to his normal self; judging from his demeanor, it appeared that no altercation had even taken place. Joy was in the air as the friends and family members talked, ate, and laughed. Perhaps Loammi had spoken with his brother-in-law and had found his right mind again.

Marine was distracted from her thoughts by the ringing of her cell phone. It was her friend Kate.

"I'd like for you and Crystal to come over to my house tonight."

A cheese and wine party with her two best friends! That sounded perfect!

For some reason, Kate and Crystal were the only friends who did not know the couple's dark secrets, as Marine had taken great care to maintain the image that her marriage was good and beautiful for them. For Kate and Crystal, Loammi was still the charming prince Marine had met more than ten years ago, and perhaps for that reason Marine had not isolated herself from them as she had from all her other friends in the Midwest. For her, dinners with Kate and Crystal were like a pause in time. She had known them for twenty years; they had traveled to France together. They were solid friendships in an ever-foreign land. They did not get together often, but when they did, it was as if time stood still. They ate their favorite cheeses, drank wine, laughed a lot, and spoke a little French. Marine had often thought, even before she became a Christian, that if heaven was but a continual evening of laughter with Kate and Crystal, it would be enough.

She made plans to go, and to bring her daughter, who would not pass up a chance to eat cheese and bread with Kate and Crystal. Marine was pleased that her children had developed a palate for French cheeses, so as to carry on her cultural traditions. In America, she had learned to cook hamburgers and Tater Tots for her family, but sometimes she missed the food that she used to eat in her youth: *soufflés*, pastries, *quenelles*, and other specialties from Lyon. She also missed the smell of French coffee brewed by her grandpa in the morning, which you could not find in this land, and the smell of fresh-baked breads and croissants coming from bakeries she walked by when she was young. Meeting Kate and Crystal was a way for her to reconnect a little bit with her roots.

By then, the evening was taking a lovely turn for both Marine and Loammi. They had made peace, and he popped in the room to let her know he had also made plans.

"Hey baby, I'm going out with my nephew. Enjoy your evening. I love you."

"I love you too, honey. Have fun."

Sealed with a kiss, the peacemaking allowed Marine to put away the bad feelings from earlier and actually go have fun with her friends. And indeed, when she returned to her sister-in-law's later that night, she was content. She put her daughter to bed and then went to lay on her own bed. Loammi had come home before she did, and he also was in a good mood.

They talked joyfully. She stroke his hand as they were talking, and suddenly she noticed something.

"Where's your wedding ring?"

"What do you mean?"

"You're not wearing your wedding ring. Why did you take it off again?"

"Uh, I don't know. It must have fallen off when I washed my hands."

Marine got up. He tried to have innocent eyes, but she knew him too well to not notice the small smirk in the right corner of his mouth as he tried to stare blankly at her. She put her jacket back on. She knew that Loammi was playing games. He had given her enough talks about the importance attached to their rings, symbols of their love for each other, and most importantly, of their vows before God. He had taken it off earlier in front of her to hurt her, to make a point—but this time it was sneaky, and he was not being honest.

She grabbed her purse.

"Where are you going?"

She reached for her coat and walked up the stairs, heading outside to the car. As she took out her key, Loammi's hand grabbed hers tightly.

"Let me go!"

"Come on, you're being dramatic; what's wrong with you?"

"I'm upset. You're not being honest with me. I'm going back to Kate's; I need to think for a while."

"Baby, you've been drinking; you're not going to take the car and drive."

Marine attempted to escape his grasp.

"You're not taking my car, bitch!"

Shocked and angered, Marine watched her hand fly as if it had a mind of its own, and she slapped Loammi across his face. She was filled with indignation. But so was Loammi. He slapped her right back, and suddenly she fell to the ground. At first it felt like someone was punching her in the back, but then she could not feel anything. All she saw was the shadow of a man pounding and pounding.

Her sister-in-law came out. Her brother-in-law. Her daughter. Someone was shouting, "Leave her alone!" Someone else "Call the police!" Marine heard sirens. An ambulance came.

As she was moved into the vehicle, she could not feel her right arm. She was shocked. Why did this happen? Why did this have to happen? Why couldn't the evening have taken a different turn? The officer sitting beside her was asking questions of his own: "What happened? How did this happen? What is your husband's name? Are those your children?"

"I slapped him first," said Marine.

Marine watched through the windows of the ambulance as Loammi got in the car and took off. She heard her son scream at him:

"Leave, and never come back!"

8

The Victim

"And Jesus answering said unto them, They that are whole need not a physician; but they that are sick. I came not to call the righteous, but sinners to repentance."

—LUKE 5: 31–32

HAVING LEFT HIS LIFE at the palace behind him, David walked far away to a city called Nob. Ahimelec the priest allowed him and his men to eat the holy bread in the temple. This charity permitted David and his men to rest.

That same day, Doeg the Edomite also happened to be in the temple, praying to God. He was a servant of Saul's, the chief of the shepherds. He must have heard David ask Ahimelec for arms, and seen the high priest give him the sword of the Philistine Goliath, whom David had defeated as a young man. Armed with his old enemy's weapon, David left for Gath, the land of King Achish, which was far from Saul. But Achish's men recognized him, and David was afraid to seek refuge with them. Since Saul was after his life, David had to use discretion and protect himself.

David continued his travels and found respite in Adullam's cave. His brothers and family who had heard of his whereabouts came to see him. It says that all the men who had financial debts and who were oppressed rallied to his side, such that he became their leader. Soon David had a small army of 400 men. With their support, David was free to move. He arrived at Moab and asked the king for hospitality in his palace. David stayed with the King of Moab, who granted him asylum until Gad the priest warned him that he *should leave and go further, into the land of Judah. So, David and his men started on a new journey that took them to the forest of Hereth.*

In the meantime, Saul was frantically looking for David. He felt betrayed by David and by all those who had taken his side. From Saul's perspective, he was the victim, and David acted as a rebellious servant by running away from him. In his eyes, he was also victimized by his son Jonathan, who had likewise turned against him. Saul was assuredly distraught to see that many defended David and even helped him to hide from him, Saul. Pleading his cause before his servants, Saul asked why no one was on his side, and why no one understood his suffering. He explained how his own son had conspired against him and turned his servant David against him. He also reminded them that he was the King of Israel, and as king he had the authority to provide for his people, unlike David.

So Doeg the Edomite, who had been in the temple with Ahimelec in Nob and had seen David with the priest, had compassion on Saul. He told him how Ahimelec had provided food and the sword of the mighty Goliath to David. Saul ordered his men to bring him the men of Ahimelec's household. When confronted, Ahimelec tried to defend David and his own actions, which reinforced Saul's self-victimization and fueled his fury. Greatly offended, the king ordered his men to kill all the priests as revenge for their treason against him. Yet the men, who feared God and knew right from wrong, did not dare to kill them. Only Doeg the Edomite came forward and obeyed the king. On that day he made eighty-five priests—servants of God—fall by his sword. But Saul's anger was not satisfied. He went on to kill the entire population of Nob.

Abiathar, son of Ahimelec, escaped and sought refuge with David in his camp. He told him of everything that had happened in Nob, which grieved David deeply and burdened him with guilt, because he had noticed Doeg in the temple of Nob that day, and he felt responsible for Saul's vindictive action. He promised to protect Abiathar. (1 Sam 21–22)

THE HOSPITAL DID A CT of Marine's cervical spine, as well as an MRI, which revealed significant cervical stenosis with spinal cord syndrome. To prevent further injury that may result in paralysis, she underwent a C3-C6 laminectomy, a surgical procedure that removes a portion of the bone to allow more space between the spinal canal and the spinal cord. She was advised to recover at a women's shelter, with her children. The numbness in her right arm faded, and she was placed in a neck cast for several weeks.

From the moment she arrived at the hospital to the moment she left for the women's shelter, Marine received hourly texts from Loammi.

Baby, I'm so sorry. I hope you're OK. I am so sorry honey. I never meant to hurt you. I do not want to hurt my wife. I love my wife. I love you, honey. I love you more than anything.

You're the most important person in the world to me, honey. I wish I could come see you and help you and help ease the pain that I have caused.

Baby, there's no greater time than this for us to heal together. We need each other, love. It is not right for a husband and wife to be separated. The Devil wants nothing else but for us to lose. I would give anything to take away the pain I've caused you and the kids. Now I know that I truly love my wife. I would give anything to be by your side right now.

My niece says the doctors say you're going to be OK. Thank God! Oh, honey, we just need each other, to heal together. I know what will cure everything that's wrong with me. It's your love. No one has ever loved me like you, baby, and God knew it would take someone like you and me to triumph in this world. I love you so much, honey. I wish you would let me show you how much I love you. You're my wife you're my wife you're my wife!

Marine dialed the phone.

"Hello?"

"I'd like to change my phone number, please."

It was mid-October in the upper Midwest. The trees still bore leaves, but their faded brown colors foretold that they would soon fall. With temperatures below ten degrees, it felt like full-blown winter rather than fall. Loammi was walking along the road, pulling his coat tight around his neck with his left hand as he supported his backpack with his right hand. The brisk wind came at him like a slap in the face that he felt he deserved. He had no real goal for the day other than look for a place where he could spend the night. How can a man who knows so many people have so few friends? he wondered. It was as if everybody hated him for what he did to his family. He understood that they would be concerned about her, about them, but somehow, he always ended up the rejected one—and that, he was certain, hurt more than physical pain.

From the moment he was born until this day, even, his life had been marked with the seal of rejection. A baby nobody wants. A stain. A black sheep among his half-brothers. His father had never questioned *their* birthright. Women came into his life and women went out of his life. Everybody was quick to say "I love you," but no one had stood by his side; even his own wife now rejected him. She must have blocked his calls or changed her number. He couldn't even hear her sweet voice nor hear the voices of his son and daughter. He was cut off, alone, again. Alone with God. As he pondered his misery, he noticed the shape of a person behaving strangely in the distance. Wait a minute. Was this person about to jump off that bridge over there?

"Hey there, hey man! Stop!"

His name was Kendrick. He had been unemployed for six months and was living on the streets and sleeping on benches, buses, and trains at night. He was weary with life. He had lost his family, just like Loammi, and wanted the pain to stop. Loammi gave him a cigarette and the man stepped down from the railing of the bridge.

"You know, man, I understand your pain, believe me. I too have lost everything, and I have no one in life but God! But you know what? God loves you. He doesn't want you to kill yourself. He doesn't want you to do that; that's a trick of the enemy. God wants you to conquer all your trials in this life. See, this world is a wicked place filled with pain and sins. And God tells us to not be conformed to this world, man, because he says that we are not of this world. We don't come from here, man; this is not our home. God is our home.

"So, in this life we can expect trials and tribulations, but God gives us the strength to endure it all! If I told you all that I have gone through in this worldly life, you would be amazed and wonder why it is that I haven't gone and killed myself! But I have endured and will continue to endure through God, who gave his only son so that people like you and me, sinners, we would have everlasting life! That means that the Devil cannot get us, no matter how much he gets us to sin. See, the Devil loves it when we sin; he laughs at our misery and our weaknesses. But God doesn't laugh. He says that if we believe in his son Jesus Christ, we shall be saved! You can't take your life, man. God has a purpose for you!"

The man backed away from the ledge, stepping forward slowly. The convulsions of his body showed that he had been moved by the words preached to him.

"Thank you, man. You have really helped me. You are a good man. You have saved my life. God bless you, brother!"

Having saved a life, Loammi felt a sense of purpose, and for a moment his sense of worth came back to him. How was it that everyone he talked to about God seemed to be touched by him, as if an angel stood by his side to anoint them instantly, but he remained an outcast? Why wasn't he cured of his demons? Sometimes he thought it was his father's fault. It couldn't have been his grandfather's because he was a preacher. They say his grandmama left her husband because he was mean to her. They say one day she got real tired of him and put a hammer in a paper bag, and hit him on the head. He survived, but that's why they separated. Loammi knew his grandma couldn't do anything wrong, and that she had to have had a reason to do what she did, but on the other hand he didn't remember anything bad about his grandpa—just the fact that he was a preacher. Sometimes he would take him to the store and buy him candy. Sometimes he'd take him to his church. His grandma and grandpa were very godly people. It was his father who had to be the cause of the family curse—mister pretty boy who loved to laugh with his lady friends and drink all day. Of course, it wasn't his fault, though; he had done his time in Vietnam and had been contaminated by that Agent Orange thing, that poison that ruined the life of many valuable black men like his dad—victims of this racist society that doesn't care about anybody's life but those with light skin.

Even now, it was so easy for people to feel bad for Marine. But if she had been a black woman, people would probably have not been so sympathetic about what had happened to her. But the white people, they are so sheltered. Even his own wife—and God forgive her because Loammi knew that wasn't her fault—but even she had not experienced any real plight in life. She did not know what it was like to be treated with disrespect every day of your life, be looked down upon, cursed at, and denied employment, just because of the color of your skin!

Marine had not experienced real suffering and still didn't understand the hypocrisy of life in America, and so instead of learning to lean on God, she listened to this white society that told her she was too good for him. That she shouldn't put up with this. The problem today was that people didn't know the power of God, and so they didn't persevere when faced with tribulations. This society had gotten too comfortable, and Marine lived in her fancy fairy tale. He, her husband, was looked down upon by society, and even though he had taught her about his plight and where he came from, she still didn't get it. And that was heartbreaking to him because he loved his wife. But she listened to everyone except him, and that hurt so much. He was her king, and she was his queen; but the queen had rejected her king. Loammi had been used to rejection all his life, and each time it hurt more than before. How could Marine be taken away from him? She was his wife. They were one in God's eyes!

THROUGH THE WINDOW, MARINE watched the snow fall, confirming the arrival of an early winter. It was peaceful at the women's shelter, and there was beauty beneath the gray skies. Surrounded by lakes, now gently frozen, the big house still offered a breathtaking view of nature, countering the cold and wind that starved any temptation to stroll along the outdoor trails. Marine did go outside often, because she was restless, and because she was allowed to smoke on the porch—which, cold as it was, gave her a moment of solace.

It was a bad habit, but the only respite from her mind. Smoking was a habit she picked up from Loammi; cigarettes smelled like him and felt like home. But also, each puff gave her a sense of feeling alive, as if the taste that filled her lungs and reached her brain allowed her a moment to focus on nothing but smoking, a moment of pure consciousness. For some reason, any thought, any discussion with others, was easier with a cigarette in hand. The other women in the shelter knew that feeling as well, because there was always someone smoking on the porch.

When she arrived at the shelter, Marine had been struck by two things. First, although they came from different walks of life, most of the women here believed in God. At the hospital, she had wanted to go to a Christian women's shelter, but it was full, and so she landed here. And yet, somehow all the women here talked about God. The second thing was that she felt lonely. When she first settled in the nine-foot-square bedroom with her two children, on beds that could not be bigger than those in a jail cell, she did not give much thought to her new routine. Her body was recovering, and she could not move her neck for a few weeks. She remembered the looks of compassion and some gazes of horror reflected in other women's eyes as they exchanged greetings. Strangers judging each other. What was she doing there?

The group meetings were informative. The women who ran the place were reliable. They clearly cared about each of the "victims," as they were called. Battered women. Somehow the term never seemed to fit her situation. After all, Loammi had problems, but he did love her. Besides, Marine did not recognize him in the abusive personality types described in the paper copies that they studied every day before dinner. Another thing that did not fit with her sensibilities was the washed-out wallpaper that ran from the stairway to the second floor, where her bedroom was; it was old and foreign. Also the yellow and beaded armchair that stood in the corner against the wall on the first floor, as if climbing one set of stairs required a break. Marine wondered how much dust it had accumulated through all those years of supporting one battered woman—one victim—after another. Marine had tried to sit in it once or twice, to find a connection with all the souls that must have walked these stairs, with all the stories these walls must have heard; she couldn't help but feel estranged. It was an old house. This was not her home. She knew it, and her daughter knew it as well. The poor thing, short of seven years old, seemed as disoriented as Marine herself, uprooted from her previous life. Luckily, her twelve-year-old son appeared to be well-adjusted. There is something to be said about the reassurance a male presence brings to women, no matter how young or old.

Slowly, they adapted. Marine got to meet some of the women. She had searched their physical appearance and psychological demeanor for what constitutes the prototype of an abused woman, comparing herself to each one of them, but there was no consensus. Some had money; others had none. Some were educated; others were not. Some had children; others did not. Some were outwardly beautiful; others were more inwardly so. Some had a charismatic personality, others were brawlers, and still others withdrawn. Yet they all shared a similar experience of a love turned sour, and that was their bond, their language, their nation. Outside of the time spent with the staff being educated about abusive relationships, the women talked about the Word of God and prayed together. Between Marine, who always had a cigarette in her hand; Jolene, who often had a curse word on her tongue; Kai, who badmouthed all men; and Lena, whose tight outfits drew much attention to her body and curves, most of the women did not look fit to preach behind a pulpit. And yet, they all held on to the truth that they experienced each in their own way: a personal encounter with Jesus. Because of that, they all had a Bible in their hands, in their hearts, or in their memories, and sought knowledge in the Word of God. Marine learned a lot about abuse and the cycle of violence, the dynamics of emotional and physical abuse at the mandatory meetings. First comes the "tension building phase," when the abuser starts feeling disturbed and negative emotions build up within him or her. Then, these triggered emotions explode and acts of abuse are carried out in the "crisis phase." Finally, the abuser, conscious that he or she has hurt his or her partner feels guilty, or fears losing her or him, so the abuser lavishes his or her partner with love and attention, luring the partner into thinking that all is well in their relationship; this is called the "honeymoon phase." That is when many women get persuaded into giving the other another chance, thinking that the honeymoon phase is proof that the perfect relationship they dream of can become reality, that the abuser can be a constant, wonderful person, if only they hang on long enough. As valuable and didactic that information was for Marine, she counted on her conversations with the women at the shelter the most, because they were about God. She was not surprised to witness the presence of the Almighty manifested in an unlikely place. God is everywhere with his children, whether they are up or down.

Marine had learned to rely first and foremost on the voice of God, which he shared with her through Scripture. But, because of her stubborn character, she had also learned to take matters into her own hands when life seemed to crumble. She needed to do something to make herself feel useful. So, after studying Isaiah's fast in the Old Testament, she decided to go on a three-day fast. She was not in the habit of fasting longer than a meal or two at a time, so that was a long fast for her. Nonetheless, she was full of hope for a miracle, and she convinced herself that it would not be that hard to tame her flesh and deny herself food for such a short period of time; after all, she was fit, and more desperate than hungry. But most importantly, if she did something for God she'd never done before, it gave her reason to hope that God would do something for her *he'd* never done before.

She made it through the first couple of days nurtured by her faith, but, at the end of the third day, she felt as if overtaken by a shadow of dread and hopelessness. Perhaps her brain was reacting to the withdrawal of endorphins, or perhaps she simply realized her spirit was not as resilient as she thought. The fact is, she felt drawn into an abyss of discouragement that showed no light behind its doors. Desperate to see the face of her Heavenly Father, she turned to him in anger: You lied to me! I loved my husband, but I did not win him by my chaste conversation. I fasted, and you did not heal the sick or break the skies open! You lied to me!

That same night, right before everyone sat down for supper, a woman handed out a pamphlet. Marine grabbed one, and it read:

God is not a man that he should lie. Numbers 23:19

With tears in her eyes, she repented, for she understood that God was by her side even though she could not see it. Though she felt pain and desperation, though her heart was broken, and though she felt incompetent to care for two children when she was in such a damaged state, God was not absent, and perhaps it was all right to not understand what he was doing, or not doing.

Marine and her two children stayed in the shelter for three months. Besides the bond that she developed with some of the women who had gone through similar experiences, she still felt lonely. It was difficult to not be home; it was hard to pass time. In its deepest sense, home to Marine was Loammi. One day, she took her children sledding with a group of other women and children looking to pass time, but her daughter started crying.

"What's wrong, baby?"

"I want to go home," she complained.

Marine did not know how to respond to her, for she herself felt lost in this strange place.

Her older brother responded, "Shut up. We can't go home. Dad hurt Mom, so Mom had to get away from him."

Because she couldn't go to work, Marine spent a lot of time talking on the phone during her time at the shelter. When she was young, Marine had experienced a lot of deep friendships— sisterhoods, even. But in the last few years, since they had moved to New York, Marine realized that she did not have many friends anymore. Was it because she had moved to the

United States? She had had a lot of friends when she was a student at the university, when she lived in student housing. Perhaps it was when they moved to New York that her circle of friends shrank. Whatever the case, she felt closer to family. So, she talked to her parents, but did so cautiously since they were extremely worried. Speaking with them ended up feeling like an ordeal, because Marine could not disclose to them how she missed Loammi and how, all of a sudden, this country that she had left them for twenty years before had become a strange land. She could not express to her mom and her siblings filled with worries for her well-being how she feared living the rest of her life without her husband. So, she made small talk. It was her duty to call them and a box to check off on her list. Truly, the person Marine enjoyed talking to the most was Loammi's uncle. Sometimes she felt that she and he were the only ones who cared about Loammi, who saw beyond the fact that he was wrong and did wrong. They were perhaps the only ones who entertained the thought that God was able to take a hold of him, and that there was hope that he would get it, that he could heal, that he would be blessed by having his life turned around.

In truth, Marine felt stuck. She had come to yet another crossroads in her marriage and was afraid to move on with her life without Loammi, but also afraid to go back to him. She was afraid that her children would be hurt by seeing her go back to him, but likewise that they would miss out by not having a father. Most importantly, she feared that if she left Loammi, she would be giving up on his restoration and would become a barren Christian without fruit. Like the mother of Linda, her former church friend, she believed that the spiritual restoration of her husband was her mission. She had heard enough stories of impenitent men turning to Christ because of the faith and prayers of their persevering wives to back up her faith and her stubbornness.

"I've seen it happen a million times!" said one of the women in the shelter to Marine.

"Really?"

"Yes. It's happened to a friend of mine. Her marriage was restored, and her husband totally changed his ways. God is a powerful god, and with faith all things are possible!"

While the staff focused on arming women with information, stressing that abusers seldom change, the fact that her comrade had heard of abusive men transformed by the power of the Holy Spirit gave Marine hope. She had already experienced faith beating the odds and did not want to give up on the power of God. She knew through Scripture that if she believed, Jesus would be able to lead Loammi to regeneration and transform his life. But as faith is evidenced by works, she needed to take a few steps in the right direction as well. Luckily, she had an ally in Uncle Jim. He was giving her regular updates from his conversations with Loammi. For weeks, Uncle Jim had been their go-between; this provided her a safety net to hold her husband accountable. After a while, she mustered the courage to talk to Loammi directly, over the phone. They exchanged short stories. Loammi was attending a program similar to Alcoholic Anonymous and appeared to be taking it seriously. He was also going to church.

From what he shared with his uncle, he was trying to do everything he could and was committed to restoring himself and his family. He was thankful Marine and the kids had a roof over their heads, even if that meant that he did not. He was glad that they were taken care of, even though he was not.

After the physical pain had left her body, an emotional kind of pain started to take hold of Marine, and she could feel its grip when she put on her clothes or served her children breakfast. It was like a stiff and over-whelming feeling of gloom that slowed her breathing and tightened her throat. A panic. Feeling stifled, she could not wait to get a chance to go outside and be slapped with the cold, but the gloom would not relinquish its hold to the blast from the north wind. Her heart now ached as her body had.

9

The Apologizer

"Then came Peter to him, and said, Lord, how oft shall my brother sin against me, and I forgive him? till seven times? Jesus saith unto him, I say not unto thee, Until seven times: but, Until seventy times seven."

—MATT 18: 21–22

DAVID GOT WORD THAT the Philistines had infiltrated the land of Judah and were fighting the Israelites in the city of Keila. He inquired of God if he should go to battle with them, and the Lord told him to go deliver Keila. David obeyed, and God delivered the Philistines unto him.

Saul heard that David was nearby. He thought that God had trapped David in Keila to deliver him unto Saul. It is interesting to see that David and Saul, though opponents, each believed that the almighty God was on his side. Saul rallied all the people to his cause, and David asked Abiathar to bring the Ephod, the priest garment that he was wearing. David asked the Lord: "Will the inhabitants of Keila deliver me into the hands of Saul?" God answered that Saul would come to get him in Keila, and that the people would indeed deliver him unto Saul.

So, David fled with his men and dwelled in the desert of Ziph, which is a mountainous land. Saul continued to look for him, but God protected David. Jonathan, Saul's son, found David and strengthened his spirit. Together, they made a covenant before God, that when it was time for David to reign over Israel, Jonathan would be by his side.

In the meantime, the inhabitants of Ziph had told King Saul that David was hiding in the mountain of Hakila, situated in the middle of the desert of Ziph. Saul blessed them for their mercy and loyalty. So, to serve King Saul and God, they searched for David and located him in the desert of Maon, then in En-Guedi.

Saul took three thousand men to hunt for David. The king descended into a plain and entered a cavern alone to rest. He did not see that David and his men were at the far end of the cavern and that he was in danger. When they saw the king alone and asleep, David's men thought that God was delivering Saul into the hands of their leader and expected David to kill his enemy. But David had mercy on Saul. He walked slowly toward the king and cut off a piece of his coat. It is said that his heart beat rapidly because of what he had done. In the ancient world, the hems of garments symbolized the status of rulers, so for David to cut the bottom part of Saul's mantel was an affront to Saul's authority as king. Though years before, Samuel had told David that he would rule over Israel and had anointed him as king, David knew that his time would come only after Saul's death, when God decided it. In the meantime, David sought to honor Saul as the true king as long as he lived. So, his gesture must have made him feel like he was taking over the throne before his time, and it filled his conscience with guilt. David told his servants that God prevented him from hurting Saul, because he was the anointed king of Israel. He forbade his men to touch him.

When Saul woke up and left the cave, David followed him and cried, "Oh my Lord, my King," and bowed before him. He tried to reason with Saul and tell him that he was not his enemy, but that he was his servant who loved him. He proved his loyalty by telling Saul that God had delivered him into his hands, but he did not kill him; David showed Saul the piece of cloth he had surreptitiously cut from Saul's coat.

Then, seemingly moved by David's voice, Saul cried and called him "my son." Saul reckoned that he had acted wickedly toward David, and that David had shown him mercy he did not deserve. He apologized for all the evil he had tried to do to him. He repented. He acknowledged that he was wrong and that David was more righteous than him. Saul ended his apology with a word of blessing, telling David that he would certainly reign over Israel one day and be a good king. At the end of his apology, Saul asked David to swear before the Lord that he would not seek to hurt him or his house, which David swore.

Saul departed and left David alone. (1 Sam 23–24)

AFTER MARINE HAD BEEN transported to the hospital and the officers had heard several sides of the story, the police started looking for Loammi.

Marine had talked to police officers, doctors, and various state workers. She had given physical descriptions and basic information about the "offender," such as the make and model of his car. Since the assault resulted in hospitalization, the sheriff's deputy in charge of the case was pursuing a felony charge. He was trying to find evidence in the medical records that there had been "breaking of the bone," which would qualify the offense at the felony level.

Since the police did not find Loammi within the three days (the legal time limit for using police resources to pursue a criminal for a second-degree assault), they stopped searching and issued a bench warrant, which would result in the offender's arrest if he was randomly picked up or if he turned himself in. Loammi was aware that there was a warrant out for his arrest. He had been warned by his uncle, who had been told by Marine, and so he asked if Marine would be willing to have the car returned to her. The arrangement was made through Uncle Jim, who facilitated the interaction without the need for the estranged couple to see each other.

Because Jim loved both parties without acrimony, he continued to act as a go-between. Being a righteous man, he could not condone his nephew's actions nor wish to help him escape their consequences, so he took Marine's side. But the fact that he shared a family bond with Loammi pulled on his heartstrings and his conscience such that he could not abandon him either. He wanted to help both Loammi and Marine heal and move forward on the path that God would lay before them, whatever it was. Jim saw Marine as a gentle albeit naïve woman who loved her husband, and she trusted him, her uncle-in-law, appreciating his counsel and respecting him as an elder. Because Marine was forlorn in a foreign land, Jim felt bound by God to protect her and give her sound wisdom. Perhaps it was also his way of making up for the fact that he had left his own dysfunctional family as a young man, and in doing so failed to step up as a father figure to Loammi when the latter was a child. Sometimes Jim's conscience troubled him, but the reality was that he had succeeded in making himself a good man. He spoke of how love should make a person feel happy and not sad. Marine and Jim agreed that Loammi was a broken man who needed to make a drastic change in his life.

"Maybe once he realizes that the has lost his family for good, he will change his ways," said Uncle Jim.

Marine replied, "I often thought that the only thing that will change him is if he were to have a near-death experience. Or if God were to come straight from the sky and tell him face to face what's wrong with him! Can you believe that I have actually prayed, several times, while we were in the midst of an argument, and Loammi was not hearing what I tried to tell him? I have prayed to God that he would send an angel to come from Heaven, right there in our bedroom, or in our living room, to speak face to face with Loammi, and tell him that he is wrong to act or speak this way."

"Well," replied Uncle Jim, "God asks that you do what *you* are responsible for in this life. Each man has a choice, and Loammi knows right from wrong, because he has been raised with knowledge of right and wrong. He knows his late grandma would not approve of his behavior; she would not side with him, and she would tell you to leave him. No one can change a man but himself."

Marine held the phone more tightly to her ear as Jim continued speaking.

"One day when I was young, I got in trouble, and they sent me to jail. That place was so terrifying that I prayed to God and told him that if he got me out of there, I promised I would never do anything again to get me back in that situation. And as the Lord was merciful to me, I have never gone back to jail in my whole life! You see, only Loammi can decide to change his ways, and if he does, you will know, because he will say the words that you have been waiting for him to say."

Marine found Uncle Jim's stories fascinating, and sometimes they spoke for hours. While they speculated and debated over what would make Loammi turn from the error of his ways, they also made a plan or two to help him in practical ways. Jim was living in an assisted care facility, being sick himself, and so he could not provide room and board to Loammi. Being without a stable housing situation is typically not conducive to the rehabilitation of someone who may need mental health treatment. Marine was conscious of that fact, having learned a lot about abusive relationships at the women's shelter, but there was nothing she could do about that. What she could do to help was gather some clothes and other belongings that Loammi had left at his sister's and bring them to Jim's, so Loammi could have gloves, a hat, winter boots, and his "big teddy bear coat," as she called it, and he would not be too cold. Aside from that, Marine's priorities were her children and herself. Loammi was wounded and hurt, but he was a man—grown and strong, capable and responsible for his actions. She knew that this separation may well be the last straw that breaks their marriage. She remembered looking at herself in the mirror at the hospital, after her surgery, and thought that she may have heard and dismissed the soft voice of the Holy Spirit in her head, whispering: "What more do you want, child?"

She knew that she had to keep herself away from another situation where she would inevitably get hurt again. But at the same time, the thought of leaving her husband for good and spending the rest of her life without him was dreadful. He had become a big part of her identity and brought sense to her life in a strange land away from the home she had left as a young woman. She had missed out on her brother getting married, on her sister moving to Paris, and on developing a relationship with her nieces and nephews. Her parents and uncles were getting older; she had disconnected from France to live a life of her own, and home was now her existence with Loammi and their children. Without him, she would be as a broken compass. Where would she steer herself?

On top of that, since she had become a Christian, Marine had devoted herself to being a dutiful wife, perhaps because deep down inside she desired to redeem herself from the mistakes she had made in her youth; or perhaps it was because Loammi had so often reminded her of those mistakes that she had made it a point to be the best wife she could be before the Lord. Perhaps at one point she had known the full absolution of Jesus, but through the years, her husband had slowly convinced her to prove her salvation with good works. It is also possible that after living with him for so long, Marine's thoughts were dominated by Loammi's, and she had become co-dependent—as long as he was not well, she could not be content. Whatever the reason, the thought of finding a new home and getting a new start without a husband beside her and a father figure for her children brought deep angst to Marine's soul, a lump in her throat and a knot in her stomach, she did not want to think about what was next for her. She wished she could just stay here and wait. Wait for a miracle; wait for life to go back to normal; wait for Loammi to be hit head-on, crushed, and remolded by the power of the Holy Spirit. So, she resolved to go through the motions of life, wait, and pay attention to which path Loammi would choose at this turning point in his life and in their marriage.

THE ATTORNEY GENERAL DENIED the felony charge, and the offense was dropped to a gross misdemeanor. At least he won't get too much time, Marine thought. And if he spends the winter in jail, he'll have a roof over his head.

But she remembered what Uncle Jim had said to her back in New York, how there is nothing more important to a man than his freedom. She knew how Loammi hated to be locked up in a jail cell, but he did not seem to understand the bondage he imposed on his own self, what with his anger and probably his resentment for his mother abandoning him at birth; perhaps a psychologist could explain what mental illness held him hostage, and set him free.

Unfortunately, Loammi had a very negative view of psychologists. He had shared with his wife that he had seen a mental health doctor at one point in his life, for his depression, and had been prescribed drugs, which he felt were not the answer to his problems. Marine had admired the way her husband had described that God's help was more powerful than prescription drugs. On the other hand, after all those years, Marine was persuaded that Loammi's problems were deeper than depression and that a psychological evaluation may help disclose them. But Loammi associated the concept of mental illness with insanity.

"I'm not crazy," he had said, every time she had suggested that he should see a therapist.

Marine had seen psychologists herself, at times when she felt overwhelmed by all her burdens. While she did not disclose her husband's behaviors—so as to not act against him behind his back—talking with a psychologist had always given her a sense of relief. But Loammi used that against her and called her "nuts," which was a good indication that he would continue to resist turning to any form of mental health therapy himself.

Of course, none of this was too big for God to handle. This time she had to step out of God's way and leave the ball in Loammi's court; all she could do was pay attention to the signs of his recovery, or his return to his manipulative ways.

Since he had her new number, Loammi texted her regularly and called occasionally. She paid attention and noticed when he expressed self-pity, and when he expressed care—when he was sorry for himself, or when he was sorry for what he had done. Uncle Jim reported faithfully to her his conversations with his nephew. Jim was like another pair of eyes, and Marine trusted him. He could confirm Marine's hope for Loammi to get better, or warn her if she was in denial. Once again, she felt that she had support, and that gave her strength.

Learning about the cycle of abuse kept Marine wondering if he would truly change, and sometimes she feared that he would not. But as time went by, Loammi showed signs of repentance.

"Please tell the kids I love them. How are they doing? What are they doing at school?"

He wanted to make sure his children were safe. He missed them, and he missed his wife. The advantage of speaking over the phone, unable to be face to face with one's opponent, is that you can disclose truths without fearing the other's reaction. Brutal honesty hurts at first, and leads to many clashes, but in the end, it is the only kind of communication that can bear real fruit. Marine found it therapeutic to share her anger with Loammi and force him to hear her side of the story.

"I never knew you felt that way," he responded. "You know that I say a lot of things that I don't mean, and you shouldn't take them all at face value."

"But I do. Words are important to me, and I take them seriously. What you tell me, I believe it."

"Honey, I have learned to fight the wrong fight. Everyone in my family has taught me that. Even my aunt. She has taught me love, but also the wrong fight. I need to overcome and learn to give it to God."

In a sense, speaking without being able to see each other was a way for the couple to get to know each other again. For Marine, it was a way to share her feelings without fear of retaliation, but for Loammi, it was a way to learn to reconnect with his wife.

Loammi was going to church and, this time, he had good things to say about his acquaintances. But Marine could not make up her mind to give him another chance or leave him for good, and her time at the women's shelter was running out. They had already extended her stay; she and the children had lived there three months, and though it was time to make a move, she felt that she was not yet ready. She had become used to the routine, and she really had all she needed: in the morning, she would get up in the small room that she shared with the two most precious people in her world, her two children. She washed up and dressed within thirty minutes, and walked through the narrow hallways of the old habitation. The washed-out colors of the wallpaper reminded her that many had walked in her path before, and she no longer felt estranged from the place. On the first floor, the women and children had breakfast, washed dishes, and greeted one another. The simplicity of this routine gave just enough purpose to her life to go on without needing to face the outside world—and her real problems.

A scholar by training, Marine enjoyed the classes. The lectures from the staff. The group discussions. The homework. Everyone gathered on the main floor in the large living room. In a sense, life had come to a halt in a way that fit nicely with her spiritual inertia and emotional denial. Later, she realized she was the type of person who hated to make decisions and had rather life make them for her. It was easier; it was a false sense of absolution in case she made the wrong decision. For how could she bear the weight of guilt if she left Loammi and he lost his family but had been genuinely repentant? On the other hand, if he did not change his ways, things could become dangerous again. She looked at the quiet pupils next to her, and down at the paper in her hands:

The tell-tale signs that your partner is manipulating your emotions.

Had she learned enough to be wiser? Could she read the signs ahead of time if the dormant volcano were to erupt again? Would she be gambling her safety by giving Loammi another chance, or would she surrender in the battle to save her husband's soul by forsaking him? Who should she listen to? Psychology? People? Friends? Loammi? Her heart? The Bible? The New Testament told the incredible story of how God changed Saul of Tarsus from a tyrant to one of the most self-sacrificing apostles, and through this narrative, Marine could foresee the Paul that her husband desired to be, and was meant to be.

"Baby, I want nothing more than to honor God and love my family. I have nothing if I can't be with my family. I long to show you—to show you all how much I love you. I have hurt you so much, and God has taken me on a journey to become a better man for my family. I have suffered the consequences of my actions. Honey, if you leave me, I have nothing to live for. Honey, I can't even see my kids, and it hurts so much."

In the end, was it the story of Saul of Tarsus that encouraged Marine to long for her husband's salvation more than her own life? Or was it that she felt conscience-stricken, as David in the Old Testament had felt when he had cut a panel off of Saul's coat? Though Loammi had hurt her, she could not bring herself to hurt him. He had become vulnerable, forlorn, and overcome with sorrow. Their family was broken; their children were seemingly adjusting to the changes of life but lacked the stability of a family and permanent home.

Marine thought about her own mother. When she was a teenager, she had asked her mom why she did not want to divorce her dad.

"We would all be so happy, the four of us, Mommy, without Dad yelling at us all the time."

Her mom had responded that it was not their fight, that she and her siblings would grow fast and live a life of their own. At other times, she had said that it was better for children to have a father, even if he is bad, than to have none at all and fill his absence with wonder and self-doubt. But deep down inside, as a teenager, Marine resented her mom for not standing up for herself. And now, some twenty years later, Marine had somehow found herself exactly where she had tried to avoid: in her mother's shoes. To some extent. Because in Marine's case, Loammi loved his family. And they believed in God. They were nothing like her parents. How could she cut off her husband from his children? How could she not give him a chance to fight for what is worth fighting for—family?

"Love, you are my wife, and you are the most amazing wife in the whole world. You are strong and you have believed in me when no one else believed in me. You could have left me a long time ago, but you stood by my side, and I have never had a love like yours. God has used you to heal me, and through you he has shown me that love is real and that family is the most important thing a man can have in life. Without you and the kids, I have nothing, and I love you guys more than anything in the world."

Marine felt compassion for him, and they started over.

They moved into a roomy townhouse in a new neighborhood in January, in the heart of winter. Loammi's countenance had changed; he was calm, and he was persistent. He spent intentional time playing with his children, taking them sledding, teaching them about God, and singing with them. He was actively looking for employment outside of his music gigs. He went back to reading his Bible. He did not put his hands on Marine again. They had made a new start, and Marine sensed that God was actively working in their lives.

10

The Adulterer

"Whoever commits adultery with a woman lacks understanding; He who does so destroys his own soul."

—Prov 6:32 (NKJV)

EVENTUALLY, SAUL RESUMED HIS *quest to kill David. He pursued him in the desert of Ziph, where David and his men were camping. Alerted by friendly sources, David planned a surprised attack on Saul's camp with his right-hand man Abischai. They saw that Saul was sleeping in the middle of the camp, surrounded by his soldiers. He had a spear beside him. Abischai tried to convince David to seize the opportunity to get rid of Saul, his enemy, once and for all, but David responded, "Do not touch him, because no one has the right to touch the anointed man of God! Only the living God can take his life."*

Instead, David and Abischai took Saul's spear as well as a jug of water to make a point. No man in Saul's camp woke up because the Almighty had put them in a deep sleep. Then, after walking to the other side of the mountaintop, David called Abner, the chief of Saul's army, and shamed him for not protecting Saul. He told him that someone had come to kill King Saul. When Saul woke up and saw that the spear and the jug of water were missing, he understood that David had had another opportunity to kill him but spared his life again. Confounded, he again repented for pursuing David. "I acted like a fool," said the king. He promised David that he would never seek to harm him again, and David gave him back his spear. David reminded Saul that God was

watching over his own life too, not just Saul's. Saul blessed him, and both men
went their way.

But deep inside, David still feared that he would one day die by the hand
of King Saul, so he fled Israel and found safety with the Philistines. He had
now six hundred men with him. They dwelled in Gath by King Achish, and
Saul ceased to pursue David. King Achish gave David the city of Ziklag, where
he and his men dwelled for a year and four months. David won many battles
for King Achish, who was pleased with him and wished to make him his ser-
vant forever. In those days, the Philistines were gathering an army to go to war
against Israel, where Saul was still king. The Philistines gathered their forces in
Shunem, and the Israelites in Gilboa.

When Saul saw his enemies the Philistines, he was taken by fear and
sought the Lord, but God did not answer him, either directly or in his dreams
or through the prophets. Confronted with God's total silence, Saul became
desperate. He asked his men to find a woman who talked to the spirits of the
dead, and consulted her in the city of En-Dor. Through all his sinfulness and
sicknesses, Saul had remained a man who worshipped God. He had even cast
out of Israel all fortune tellers and all worshippers of false gods. So, when Saul
decided to consult a fortune teller, he was rejecting all of the principles that he
had adhered to his whole life; this was a huge turn of events and a complete
breach of character. One could say he turned to the dark side and committed
adultery against God, as Israel had before him.

Saul went through with his infidelity against God; at nighttime, he dis-
guised himself and traveled with two of his men to consult the witch. (1 Sam
26—28:10)

IN FRANCE, AS MARINE remembered, spring announced itself with the fresh
smell of rain. Not the kind of rain that licks the filth off the pavement before
springing up to your nostrils, but the kind of rain that cascades down the
trees, gets trapped in the buds forming on the branches, lingers for a few
seconds as if savoring a moment of lovemaking that it knows will not last,
and when it must let go, reluctantly drops its tears on the grass. In the morning, those tears that are called "dew" bear the cost of their happy memories
as they are scorched away by the sun taking over another day. It foretells a
new beginning, but new beginnings made Marine think that something was
always left behind.

In the upper Midwest of the United States, Marine recognized spring
from the smell of the snow melting. It was time to open the windows and
doors that had been sealed for months and let in the cool air, which carried a
scent of plain water, like that of a clean, crisp brook. Her family was learning

to enjoy their new and quiet neighborhood, away from traffic yet within walking distance of everything: schools, stores, gas stations, restaurants. Inside, they still lived among boxes and disorganized spaces, but it looked nothing like the chaos they had come out of. It was a new start. The school year would soon end, and they had great plans for the summer, including spending a lot of time with their children to build new, happy memories; they planned to spend their time swimming, fishing, playing in parks, and laughing. Those were their favorite activities. In New York, by the coast, they had bought fishing poles—fulfilling one of Loammi's dreams—and had started a habit of driving to a lake on those lazy Sundays. Once again, they were eager to continue to build on those moments. Loammi took pleasure in reminding his family how to strategically put bait on the hook and wait for a bite. The children got very excited when they caught a fish, big or small, and occasionally, Marine was able to cook what they caught. She was not sure how clean the lakes were, but it was not the moment to encourage Loammi to be suspicious of an activity he had set himself up to cherish with his children. Soon the kids would leave for the rest of the summer to go visit their grandparents in France, so their parents were trying to make up for the pain that they had put them through and replace sad images with happier ones.

The day came when Loammi and Marine drove to Chicago to put their children on the plane. It was a direct flight to Geneva, and from there, Marine's parents would pick them up and drive them across the French border to their hometown, just a couple of hours away from Switzerland. It was the cheapest and fastest way to fly, and they had done it before. Driving to Chicago, of course, had a way of bringing Loammi and Marine closer. This time, coming back home without their children was the beginning of a second honeymoon for the couple, who had not been alone together in over a decade. So, they got to know each other again and learned to pay attention to each other's likes and dislikes. They had time to talk, watch movies—just the two of them—and have long conversations. They found a bond even in sharing chores. They went on a few adventures. They visited antique shops and a quaint family-owned store that sold old toys Loammi had not seen since he was a child, they went out to new restaurants and Marine made her husband eat oysters, paying homage to the ocean in New Jersey and to her childhood vacations by the saltwater bays in northern France. Every day, the agenda was to enjoy life. One day, Loammi decided to pay his good friend Mitch a visit, except that, this time, he invited Marine to come along.

Mitch lived in a modest mobile home that he had renovated over the years, at times with Loammi's help. Their friendship dated back to years before Loammi met Marine. When they pulled up to the driveway, Marine realized how long it had been since she had been there. Years, for sure. Yet everything looked more or less the same, as if time held still the peacefulness of this home: the same white façade albeit with an extension, the same screen door, the same Mitch standing behind the door that inevitably opened before you had a chance to knock. Smiling, welcoming, inviting.

"Do you want something to drink? Something to eat? Make yourselves at home!"

Marine and Loammi sat together in an armchair in front of the seventy-five-inch TV screen, with Mitch sitting comfortably in his own armchair on the other side of the room. Though the windows did not let much light in, the place felt cozy.

"What've you been up to, man?"

"Same old. The kids are in France right now, so Marine and I have the place to ourselves. What about you?"

"Oh yeah. Maybe we should all move to France soon, because it's getting real ugly in this country."

"I keep telling her. Armageddon is coming, and it's hitting here first!"

The two men laughed.

Mitch looked at Marine. "So, is the government as crooked in France as it is here? I hear people are in the streets again."

Marine smiled. Sitting comfortably on her husband's lap, she proceeded to tell Mitch about her home country and compare the cultures of the two nations. Loammi's hand tightened around her waist. He was smiling, proud of his wife—"the professor"—lecturing his friend. Though she never did become a professor at the university, he continued to refer to her in that way. Being there in that moment, Marine felt included again in her husband's life, like she did at the beginning of their relationship.

WHEN THE KIDS RETURNED from their vacation, they had a lot of stories and memories to share. They were excited and happy. Soon, life got busy again with the preparations for the upcoming school year. All was well and peaceful. This time, it was as if their former troubles had disappeared and sought to be forgotten.

While Loammi had developed practical steps to control his emotions and impulses, such as walking away when he was upset, he started getting obsessed with conspiracy theories. Throughout his life, he had cultivated an interest in those sorts of things, studying signs that governments and celebrities had sold their souls and were subliminally working a new world order that most people—being too gullible and desensitized—were oblivious to. But for some reason, he began to believe that this particular year was *the* time to pay attention. Loammi had convinced himself that this coming year was surely going to set in place the mark of the beast, and it would be impossible to buy or sell anything without selling your soul. He only had a few months to store the necessary materials for himself and his family before he resigned to a life of poverty, with nothing more to gain from this world. Since the Devil was going to make it impossible for him to have any more possessions, he wanted to be ready. After all, his spirit had always been good at discerning evil, and this knowledge made him feel that he had the upper hand over the End Times: by following his instincts, he would avoid being caught unprepared. He would have no regrets.

Like before their life in New York, her husband's fascination with evil still bothered Marine. She did not like it when he made the kids watch videos about the Illuminati or other hidden signs that the Devil was behind the most subtle things. She agreed with her husband that in the invisible spiritual realm, demonic angels were roaming and able to influence human beings, but as surely as she believed that, she relied on the logic that if one-third of the angels had fallen, then for every wicked angel, there were twice as many good angels from God. Knowing that the almighty God was all-powerful was enough for Marine to live carefree in an evil world. But not so with Loammi.

One evening, Marine was sitting on the sofa, darning a sock that had a hole in it. She liked to sew torn fabric back together; it reminded her that mistakes can be corrected, and sins can be covered. Loammi interrupted her concentration with a strange question.

"What would you think if I left to go do something evil for a time, to make all the money I can, and then came back and never did it again?"

Marine took a moment to think. Somehow, she did not ponder what he was trying to say, but rather why he would say something like that. Though Loammi had found a second chance with his family, Marine could tell that he was still not happy. It seemed that he was dragging a chain behind him. Broken dreams. Life for a man is more than a happy family; a man who does not accomplish goals and feats withers away. Though on the outside they seemed to have triumphed over the vicious cycle of abuse, Marine knew the angst in her husband's soul. She often felt it in her own stomach when she looked at him: smiling on the outside, but dissatisfied on the inside. He had not made anything of his music, and his dreams of success were passing him by. No matter how much she tried to build him up, he was not where he wanted to be. She had what she needed, but he did not. He was not the provider. He was not successful. While men his age were looking for more opportunities to grow in their businesses, their experiences, or their knowledge, he did not even have the basics down. Was he thinking of robbing a bank? Was he having a midlife crisis?

"I think this is something between you and God," she responded.

It would have been easy for her to tell Loammi: "Please definitely, certainly, do *not* go do something foolish and hurtful that you will regret. Resist the Devil; turn to God. Honey, pray about it; you don't want to do wrong." but she had learned that he had to take responsibility for his actions, and she could not hold him back by trying to be his conscience. She said nothing and kept on sewing. So much so that she thought nothing of it the next day, or the next, or the next. Until one day, when Loammi did not come home.

Perhaps he was out with his friend James and had fallen asleep at his studio. Occasionally, he disappeared for almost twenty-four hours making music with his friends. So, Marine did not try to contact him, but deep down she felt that something was wrong. She tried to lean on God and read Psalms to quiet her spirit. She wanted to conquer the fear that had been her captor since New York and rediscover in herself the woman warrior God had made her to be, the faithful servant that she was when she believed in everything and feared nothing. When she had first become a Christian.

The next day, thirty-six hours after Loammi had gone missing—and since she had last talked to him—she decided to send a text.

Are you all right or should I call the police to look for you?

An hour later he texted back, *I'm OK.*

He came back in the evening, kissed his children, and ate with them. Then he took Marine for a drive.

"Look, I'm not getting any younger, and I need to provide for my family. If I got sick and died, what would you all have from me? Nothing. So, I'm going to do some things and be gone, and I don't want you to ask me questions about it."

"What are you going to do? Where are you going? For how long?"

"I can't tell you, and I don't know for how long. But when I'm done, I'll be back home, and we'll be OK."

Marine did not like what she heard. She wanted to grab her husband and give him the hope that was in her heart, the contentment that she experienced after bringing her fears to the feet of Jesus, and the promise that everything would be all right if he just leaned on God. But she had no such authority. It was his battle, and she shut up.

AFTER THAT NIGHT, NOTHING was ever the same again. The next two years turned out to be the greatest test of faith that Marine ever had to endure. First it started with Loammi being gone most of the time, and then more, and more again. He would come and grab some clothes and musical instruments and take them out of the house. Then he grabbed his computer. And the rest of his clothes. Pretty soon his entire studio was gone from their house. It was as if everything that was his essence had disappeared. The only thing that he did not take was his Bible, and that grieved Marine. She was starting to get reacquainted with loneliness. She felt abandoned, and disconnected from reality; she did not understand what was going on. He texted very rarely. She was scared. All sorts of scenarios were going through her mind. Was he dealing drugs? Had he joined a gang? Was he a criminal? Was he cheating?

She spent most of her days confused, as if living in a haze: going through the motions of taking care of her children, playing with them, going to work, and interacting with people. But at the end of her days of public masquerades, she could not wait to be alone with herself and cry, to face the desperate thoughts that she had dismissed all day and bring them before God. "Lord, you know all things; please keep my husband safe and sane. Please reach out to him and lead him back to You."

Then one day, she got a call from him, late in the evening.

"Baby, I just want to tell you that no matter what happens, you are the love of my life, and I will always love you."

Perhaps a less selfish woman would have feared that he was about to commit a crime that would lead to his death, and cry out to God for his protection. But for some reason, she wondered if he was being unfaithful. As if it was better for her to have an ending worthy of a Greek tragedy, where love is greater than death, and the hero proclaims his love before he dies, than to have him betray the only thing that had remained pure in their marriage, she feared the latter. Actually, Marine had had suspicions all along that this time Loammi really was cheating on her, but it took a long time to find out what was truly happening.

One day, Loammi walked into their apartment with a grin on his face. As usual, he had new clothes on. Clean, well-pressed. His skin glowed, and his cologne filled in the air. He walked in as if he owned the room. Confident. Though Loammi, as a musician, always liked to dress well and was charismatic in public, Marine thought something had changed about his countenance over the last months. Beneath his appearance, she could no longer see the simple man who liked to build things with his hands and scrub down at home. His newfound arrogance was that of a different man.

"I have something to show you all."

"Mom, look, Dad got us a new car!"

That day, Marine never saw with her eyes the new black Cadillac Loammi came to show off, but her children described how roomy and clean it was and how good it smelled, after their dad took them for a ride. Her son was impressed.

"I think Dad has never provided for us like that. This time he is taking care of us more than ever!"

What could Marine say? How could she explain to him, a young man finally proud of his daddy, her resistance and suspicion—the opposite perception he had of her husband? Loammi, on the other hand, understood the defiance in her eyes.

"Let's go for a walk!" he commanded.

In the cold with their hands hanging at their sides, they climbed the snowbanks across the railroad tracks and reached the park behind their home; somehow this trail they had strolled many times before had lost its familiarity. In her husband's absence, Marine had realized a newfound selfishness. She did not care one bit that he came home with money and presents, or that she was a killjoy who did not support his accomplishments when he showed off to the kids. She wanted to rip up this picture and confront him. Only one thing mattered to her at that moment:

"I want to know the truth. Are you sleeping with another woman?"

Loammi sighed and looked up at her, before finally stating: "No, I am not messing with no woman. And why is this what you're thinking anyway? You're so selfish!"

Typically, a woman knows those things, but Loammi had always been skilled at the art of persuasion, and once again Marine felt confused. Could he be telling the truth? Was there any chance, no matter how small, that he was not guilty as presumed, but innocent? If that was the case, that would make *her* the guilty one for falsely accusing him. Even she, no matter how much her conscience troubled her, wanted to believe him. How could she know for sure? For the next few weeks, Marine lived with this obsessive quest for the truth, and it consumed her thoughts. She begged God to send her clear, unequivocal signs. And the signs were sent.

One day, she was driving back from the store with her now eleven-year-old daughter in the back seat. Exiting the parkway, Marine drove to the intersection. The light was green, so she looked to her left at the cars stopped in opposing traffic, and she noticed the black Cadillac. She recognized the man in the driver's seat. But she did not recognize the woman sitting next to him.

"Look, Mom, it's Daddy's car!"

As she watched the couple, a wicked thought ran through Marine's head: let's see how you're going to explain this to your child! Without shame, she honked the car horn loudly. He turned his head, and she honked again. He saw her, but her light turned red, and his light turned green, so the black Cadillac took off. Marine was angry, surprised, and still confused. The woman did not seem particularly pretty. She was no showstopper. The other detail that struck her was that Loammi's face lit up with a smile while he talked to that woman. He seemed to enjoy his conversation, and that further fueled the fire of jealousy burning in her. She had no time to waste, or she would lose them; as soon as she was able to, she turned right and squeezed through the traffic, proceeding to chase the Cadillac with minimal care for safety. It was still in sight, and she had to speed up. As she got closer, she honked the horn again.

"Mommy, why is Dad not stopping?"

Marine continued to press the right pedal as well as the horn on her steering wheel to get her cheating husband's attention until she understood that her car was no match for that brand new Cadillac. Somewhere on the freeway, she lost the mad chase. Suddenly, she remembered that her daughter was in the vehicle with her.

"Don't worry, baby," she said. "Dad didn't see us because he must have been playing music loud as usual. He must be busy going to work or something. That's OK."

But it was not OK for Marine. Now more than ever she had to find out who that woman was and what her husband was doing with her. But she had to do so without involving the children in the mess. So, when Loammi called a few minutes later, she at least had the sense to pull over in a parking lot and get out of the car.

"Hey, this is not what it seems," Loammi said softly.

"Really? It seems very clear to me what's going on."

"I'll see you guys later." Loammi seemed determined to wipe the slate clean, but Marine was likewise determined to throw evidence in his face.

"I don't care. As you make your bed, you sleep in it . . . with whoever you choose!"

Somehow hanging up on him seemed to provide some relief and a false sense of victory. Yet she was still confused and now engaged in a mental chase for the truth; she had to eliminate all possibilities that she was wrong about this before she could truly accuse her husband. So, she looked for evidence. When cleaning their bedroom, she found a letter on the floor, in a pile of music magazines. The letter was a traffic fine that had been paid by a woman whose name Marine did not recognize. At first, she thought perhaps that was a relative she did not know about, but when she saw that one of the magazines had an address with the same name on it, she understood that that was where Loammi was living—at that woman's address. Not willing to leave her children wondering of her whereabouts after work, she waited for the weekend to leave her home. Then she drove to the address.

It was a quiet neighborhood not very far from where they lived. As she got closer, Marine's right leg started to shake on the pedal. Led by her obsession, she pushed through her fear and shame and slowly drove by the address number, and there she saw it: the black Cadillac, parked in the alley in front of the garage door. It was a two-story house with a basketball hoop on the façade next to the garage door. The woman had children. Marine already knew that, because she had Googled her and found out quite a bit about her: divorced, with a boy and a girl aged about the same as her own children. She owned the house and had a good job, as well as a good reputation. What was she doing with her husband, and did she know he was married? Or was she fooled by him?

FOR ABOUT A YEAR, Marine took a walk on the dark side. Bottles of beer piled up on the counter on the weekends. She often fell asleep on the couch. Her son, then a junior in high school, was very invested in his friends, which made it easier for her to not be as present-minded. Her daughter, still in middle school, needed more of her time, and she struggled to be a mom. And a dad. It was hard to find solace in the Word of God. The days repeated each other.

Obsessed with her husband's whereabouts, Marine started listening to his phone messages. Up until then, they had had complete trust, so she knew the password to his voicemail. The first few times she accessed his messages, she did feel like she was doing something wrong and forbidden. But even God warns that jealousy is stronger than the grave, and her emotions took over. At first, there was nothing incriminatory. Several messages from men and women. One from a pastor. Loammi must be innocent. Some women called him "baby," but they could be family members or long-time friends. There was no way he could cheat with several women—that would be crazy. There was also an old message from her, which he had not erased.

Feeling guilty for invading her husband's privacy, Marine limited her investigations to a couple of times per month. Just enough to keep reminding herself that he may not be cheating, that he still loved her. She tried to focus on the Word of God, but it did not take her mind off Loammi. And one day, she heard the words that she feared: "I love you." A gentle feminine voice in Loammi's voicemail. She had left messages before. She sounded like a white woman. Was she the woman living at that house? Why were there still messages from other women? One of them had a particularly coy voice. Could Loammi have several mistresses?

Marine had never felt like that before. Obsessed. Somehow she was consumed by anger and desperation. She plotted; she could not let Loammi know that she listened to his messages, lest he change the password to his voicemail and she lose total control over his life. His actions hurt, but she felt that knowing nothing would push her into the abyss. She had to do it, or die. She organized the pieces, searching for her home, her children, Loammi, and herself, in this puzzle. Denial. Delusion. Why had he become everything?

Soon she sort of stalked the other woman, calling her number and hanging up, driving by the house with the address she now knew well. One day, she knocked on her door just to see what she looked like. And mark her territory.

"Hello . . . " A woman answered the door. She seemed friendly, but looked plain.

"Are you Izzie?"

"Yes . . . And who are you?"

"You don't want to know who I am." Marine walked back to her car.

After that encounter, she realized her powerlessness over the situation. One morning she felt the tug of madness pulling her down.

"Jesus, Jesus, Jesus, Jesus, Jesus . . . "

Marine spent months vacillating between her faith in God and her human nature. She left desperate messages on her husband's cell phone, hoping they would make him feel guilty. She cried to God. First praying, then shouting at him. But nothing made her feel better. She was obsessed with her pain. For a Christian, suffering is bearable as long as it has a purpose in Christ. Now, Marine saw that what she had endured all those years for this man whom she could hardly call her husband anymore would be for nothing; all of a sudden, her life had spiraled into absolute pointlessness as her marriage was disintegrating anyway. She felt pitiful.

Then one day, Loammi made his run home, as he did once in a while to bring gifts and money and see his children. He was shaving in the bathroom, making himself pretty and ready for his evening plans, whatever they may be, all the while having a distant conversation with his wife—a monologue, rather. As he was talking, he ended up revealing his own crisis of faith.

"Honestly, I don't know what I believe in anymore," he said. "I don't even know if that Jesus stuff is true after all."

These words shook Marine to her core, and from that day on, she understood that there was a battle for her husband's soul. It did not take away her pain, but it helped her refocus, and relinquish control to God. That year was the second year of Loammi's absence, and Marine devoted all her forces to dive more deeply into the spiritual realm than she ever had before.

In those days, the family did not have a church to go to, so Marine read the Word of God by herself. She started with Matthew 17, then Isaiah 58. She took to heart that fasting was another thing she could do to cry out to Heaven. It gave her a sense of purpose, as opposed to inertia. From then on, she enjoyed nothing but studying the Bible. While she had to continue to be a mother to her children, a colleague to her coworkers, and a neighbor to her neighbors, she withdrew in the spiritual sense. Her only sense of feeling alive came from reading the Word of God and debating it with him. In Isaiah 1:18, God calls this "reasoning" with him.

Marine had entered fighting mode, and God was slowly pulling her from her abyss, giving her hope, somehow. Hope that he still loved her. She read blogs about women sharing stories similar to hers, and suddenly she no longer felt alone. Loammi's absence still weighed on her, but it did not crush her. She understood that there was a purpose greater than a marriage and greater than a happy life on this earth. She saw that her husband had turned away from his faith, from the one thing that he had believed in all his life, no matter how wrong or right he had been; the only rock in his being had been kicked to the curb and knocked down. He was willfully committing various sorts of sins that he knew were against God. This was a compete departure from everything he held dear and everything he had been.

11

The Con Artist

"Keep yourselves in the love of God, looking for the mercy of our Lord Jesus Christ onto eternal life. And of some have compassion, making a difference: And others save with fear, pulling them out of the fire; hating even the garment spotted by the flesh."

—JUDE 21–23

BY TURNING TO WITCHCRAFT, Saul's continual disobedience of and rebellion against God had reached its climax. Not hearing from God, Saul sought guidance elsewhere. One can assume that Saul turned to dark powers out of desperation, fulfilling the universal human reaction to keep on doing wrong when we fear we have gone too far to turn back.

Fully conscious of his impending sin, King Saul disguised himself to see the fortune teller. She had been banished from Israel for practicing witchcraft—as a result of his own decree—and he didn't want her to recognize him. Did he mask his identity to hide from her, or to alleviate his conscience toward God? Did he think he could get away with sin?

When the witch summoned the spirits, the prophet Samuel appeared to her, and she understood the true identity of her client. "Why have you deceived me?" she asked. Does a con man feel guilty? Was Saul ashamed or angry at being caught, like a criminal is who does not regret his sin but hates to do the time? Only God knows the true intent of a person's heart, and that is likely why he calls us not to judge one another.

Disturbed, Samuel's spirit admonished King Saul, reminding him how far he had fallen. He reminded him that because he had failed to obey God and destroy Amalek, God had left him, and Samuel himself had foretold the king that the eternal God would take away the kingdom of Israel from him and give it to David. Samuel finished by telling Saul that the next day, he and his sons would be delivered to Israel and killed.

Overcome by the horror of what Samuel had revealed to him, Saul lost his appetite. The witch and Saul's servants had to reason with him so he would eat before leaving. (1 Sam 28:11–25)

LOAMMI HAD ALWAYS HAD a way with words. Since he was very young, he remembered how easy it was to cover up his mistakes by altering or distorting the truth just a little bit. Oh, not much, he just had to stretch a few lines of veracity and not disclose all the details to others. He guessed that did not *technically* make him a liar. Sitting on a bench with a bottle of water in his hands, he tilted it sideways and observed how the water changed form as it filled one side of the bottle, then the other.

In fact, he did not like to lie. When asked a question, he would never give a straight-up "no" if it was true, or "yes" if it was false, because God hates lying, and the Devil is the father of all lies—and Loammi did not want to side with the Devil. So, he came up with a tactic that he used over and over. He found that it was fairly easy to redirect a topic of conversation so the interrogator lost track of what he or she originally wanted to ask, and with that tactic he had preserved his integrity. People were so gullible anyway; it was unbelievable how quickly they were willing to believe what they wanted to hear. Women, especially so. To Loammi, most women were simple. They were so easily charmed, desperate even, so much so that it didn't take much to set them up as pawns on a chessboard. But he didn't want to treat his wife like that; she was not like that. She was special and did not deserve the pain of that chess game. Lord knows he had hurt her enough; it was better to leave her out of that one.

There were, however, more complicated women—the type who insisted on getting straight to the point, who had found a little shadiness behind his eyes—but he had found another way to bring them back to his side: by accusing them of setting him up, thus turning the tables against them.

Truth be told, Loammi did not enjoy playing the con man. He had learned to use those skills as a young man, but it brought him no real satisfaction, and he knew it was wrong. In fact, deep down, he was ashamed of himself and of the women who were so simple-minded, and to some extent, as guilty as himself for going along with this masquerade of being falsely wooed. In fact, he had noticed that people in general were quick to change their ways and their principles just like that, both for profit and to gain an advantage. So, in a sense he was not doing any more wrong than anyone else at any given time. He was simply on a level playing field with most people with whom he came in contact.

If not confronted about his excuse, whether by a sharper mind or his own, his argument would stand as long as he needed it to accomplish his purpose. Because he had set something in motion, and it was bearing fruit, he would play the game for a little while. People were getting what they wanted from him anyway, and he made sure he would also get what *he* wanted.

"Here you go, sir! Your oil is changed."

The mechanic handed him the key to his black Cadillac.

"Thank you, man!"

Loammi opened the door and got into the vehicle as a man of means. His brand-new car still had that 'new car smell'! A little music: his self-made tracks played like a charm through those amplified speakers. Loammi wasn't a star measured by the world's standards, but he was his own star! In his eyes, he was a champion! And so he was in every other women's eyes as well, with his good looks and his music skills. He had even gained the respect of men! He was convinced that his own wife thought of him that way as well. He had dreamed of offering his wife and kids everything they desired. He had dreamed of bringing home so much money that his wife wouldn't have to work if she didn't want to—that he would provide—but somehow things had not worked out like that for him. Therefore he had had to take great measures and cut some corners, and that was not the way he had envisioned living—that was not God's prescribed way to a blessed life. Yet the only damnation that felt real to him then was dying and leaving his family with nothing.

When he stopped by the house to bring a brand-new TV or a hundred-dollar bill, new school supplies or clothes for the children, they were happy. It was clear to him that they were finally proud of their dad! The gratification that he felt from seeing their welcoming and surprised faces made up for the fact that he could not face Marine's unuttered reproach and condemnation. However, these days, she *was* making an effort to hold her peace. In fact, she had been so serene the last time he had been over, he had almost wanted to spend one night at home. But he couldn't, because he was not going to play her. When he came back home, it would be for good.

Sometimes he wondered if he had crossed the line and, perhaps, he could not come back home. Maybe Marine would not take him back this time, or maybe he would not find his way home. Perhaps he had crossed the line with God too. And if that was the case, then he might as well keep doing what he was doing; there would be no sense dwelling on it anymore. He was just a man, and by definition, an imperfect being. God had to know that.

Loammi's reflection was interrupted by a text message from his main girlfriend.

Hi baby, I'm on my way home. Don't forget we're going to dinner with my friends tonight!

Loammi sighed. Act III. The show must go on.

MARINE HAD LEARNED A lot from the book of Hosea. It brought her comfort to see the hand of God in Hosea's life; she identified with the pain that the prophet's adulterous wife, Gomer, put him through. The more pages she turned, the more wet—almost slimy—her hands got from wiping her nose because she had run out of tissue and did not want to put the book down. She remembered that Loammi used to tell her that in the years when he was a young Christian, he would spray his best cologne in his Bible. It was true; if she picked it up right at that moment and opened it, it still smelled like Versace. God forgive her if she handled his Word with grimy hands that had been wiped off on her jeans.

She got up and washed her hands, all the while thinking about Hosea. She had underlined every other paragraph and decrypted each moment of Gomer's adulteries and Israel's sinfulness, matching each sequence with Loammi's state of mind. She had read how God asked Hosea to name his last son "Loammi," a name marked by God's rejection of Israel, declaring, "for ye are not my people and I will not be your God" (Hos 1:9). Marine believed that she felt toward her husband exactly as God had felt toward Israel—whom he mentions as his bride—and Hosea against his wife Gomer, for all loved their spouses and were equally betrayed. So, from that day on, she decided to change her husband's name on her phone to that of "Loammi." He would be a "Loammi" until he returned to God; until the Lord brought him to the valley of Jezreel to heal him and then return him home where he belonged, as in the book of Hosea, until he was made whole like Gomer, because Marine thought that that would be her story. She was inspired by the book of Hosea and believed that as the prophet Hosea had witnessed the redemption of his wife by the hand of God, she would likewise witness the transformation of her husband by Jesus. Marine had read how God planned to strip the whoredoms off of his bride Israel and turn even her lovers against her, so she would have no one to run to; and once he got her alone, God would build a hedge around her, and she would remember him, and sing a new song to him. As this happened with Israel, and with Gomer, in her mind, Marine saw this happen with Loammi.

Fasting became a way of life for Marine. It became easier and easier to fast for long periods of time. While she grew to understand that nothing she did would press the hand of God, Marine felt that if she did not do something, she would fall under the darkness of insanity, because all she could think of when she woke up was how unbelievable it was that this is where she was in her life, this is what her husband was doing, and this is where they were—that her hard work and sacrifice to build a family and her endurance to save her husband's soul had resulted in nothing good. It was as if a gulf had opened up the earth, and she did not see it coming. She did not recognize who she was in this alternate reality, and the only anchor that she had was Jesus.

"Mom, are you fasting today? Can I fast too?"

Children have pure hearts. Her daughter could see that her mom was no longer angry, but hopeful—that she held onto God for provisions and safety, and as a consequence, she was stronger and mentally more stable. She could see that God could be trusted and answered her own prayers by making her mom happier. Marine allowed her to fast for one day. But in the afternoon, the little girl broke down crying.

"What's wrong, honey?

"I don't know, Mom. I just feel really sad."

"*Ma chérie*, you did very well fasting all day, but you are too young to fast anymore. God must be very pleased that you wanted to sacrifice food to hear from him. But when you start feeling bad, that means it's time to eat."

Because Marine had to protect her children, she did not want to encourage her daughter to follow in her footsteps. In fact, she hoped that her daughter would never have to go through any of the ordeals she had had to go through. She wanted her children to have a normal life, but hers seemed so far from the norm, that she could not enjoy anything anymore, not even food. Was she taking things too far? Where was she bearing fruit in her life? No miracles were happening. She wasn't converting anyone. She was just standing, that's all. Was she just useless as a Christian? Would she end up dying from her own stubbornness? Am I just a fool? she wondered.

Sometimes, when Marine was stuck, she found nothing better than giving God an ultimatum. She wanted a clear answer. As she had a routine medical appointment coming up, she prayed: "Father, I don't know what I'm doing. If it is pleasing to you that I keep fasting, then say it through the mouth of the doctor. Otherwise, if you want me to stop, have him tell me to stop." The interesting part of these rare moments when she "demanded" a response from God was that it liberated her faith to expect an answer.

At her visit, she told the physician that she had been fasting for a while, and he replied:

"That is a very good thing to do! Because when you fast, everything in you that wants to be alive fights to stay alive."

Having heard from God through the doctor and feeling supported by him, Marine started worrying less about herself. She focused her energy on being joyful around her children and enjoying their presence—on not lashing out at Loammi, though he still stirred up anger in her heart every time she saw him. She kept her mind on his salvation. One evening, he came home and had been drinking. He cursed at God. Shuddering, Marine saw a trapped and hurt soul, so she instinctively repented on his behalf. Then, she heard the Spirit of God whisper gently, "You see, he treats me the same way he treats you."

All right, Lord, she responded in her mind, I will keep loving him like Hosea loved Gomer, because I know him too well and I want to see his salvation.

Though she had much to be thankful for in life, and many women would have advised her to do otherwise—to grow a backbone and dump that loser, to go live her life with her wonderful children whom she loved very much, that she could easily find a better man, that she didn't have to put up with all his BS, that she was worth more than that—Marine was living with a hole in her heart, and God knew that. He knew that she was not whole, and he also knew that she was not ready to give up on her dream of seeing her husband restored. Because God is such a gentle spirit, he cares about our deepest desires. Marine wanted a fairy tale ending and was not ready for the ending God had foreseen, so he gave her time.

IN THE MEANTIME, LOAMMI finally had what he thought was the one thing he was missing in his life: access to money. No matter what anyone says, success is measured by status on this earth, and respect is given to he whose pockets are deepest. Loammi saw the difference in how he was now received when he stepped out of his car. No one ever jumped to serve him when he drove his old family car, that piece of junk that he had to keep fixing. But when he and his girl went to a retreat up north in the heart of white America, he was greeted like a gentleman. "Hello, sir. How can I help you?" "Right away, sir." Yes, even racist America finally looked at him with respect.

In addition to the relief of not stressing about whether next month's rent could be paid, or wondering if he would have to pawn his new drum set, Loammi found a new freedom in being able to afford things—an addiction, even. At first, he was satisfied with being able to bring home a hundred-dollar bill and provide for his kids. But quickly, he enjoyed being able to buy name-brand jeans for himself, expensive shades, and good skin products. He never ran out of cologne, and he looked so sharp! He could get new musical instruments. Right now, he even had his eyes set on a motorcycle. Of course, it all came at a price. Deep down, he despised having to put on a mask everywhere he went, spending time with his main girlfriend's family, having to answer questions. Sometimes people were just so darn nosy! Why did they want to know everything about him? At first it was easy, because he knew that the part he played was not the real him. But gradually, it was taking a toll on his spirit, playing so many parts with different people. Girls wanted more from him; people asked more questions. Sometimes all he wanted was to be left alone!

One day, Loammi could not bear the guilt of his conscience or the absence of his children. He longed to be at peace with the woman who loved him unconditionally. He wanted to open the Word of God without feeling like a hypocrite. And most of all, he didn't want to be condemned for his sins. Not all the money in the world was worth losing your soul over, and he knew that. How many times had he quoted Matthew 16:26 to his children? So, he finally came back home.

12

Death

"Do not be deceived; God is not mocked: for whatever a man soweth, that shall he also reap."

—GAL 6:7

BEFORE THE UPCOMING BATTLE *against Israel in Jizreel, the princes of the Philistines complained to King Achish that David should not accompany them because he was formerly in Saul's army and was likely to betray them; so, King Achish bade David to leave the region. The request saddened David, who left in the morning with his men, and returned to Ziklag, where he dwelled. But upon arrival, he found that while he and his men were gone, the Amalekites had destroyed the city and taken every woman and child captive. The people started to turn against him, and David was in great distress. It is said that he leaned on God, asking him if he should pursue his enemies, and God told him yes.*

So, David pursued his enemies to their camp, where the Amalekites were eating, drinking, and dancing—celebrating their great victory over the camp of the Philistines. David and his army attacked, waging a battle against them from morning to evening. Only four hundred men escaped his sword and his anger. David set free all the women and children that had been taken from his camp, and recuperated all the goods that had been stolen. David shared his gain with all his Philistine friends.

Meanwhile, on the mountain of Gilboa, the war was going well for the Philistines, who were picking off the fleeing Israelites. As prophesied by Samuel, the Philistines killed all of Saul's sons: Jonathan, Abinadab, and Malchishua. Short of being killed himself, Saul received a deep wound. Afraid to be taken alive and tortured by the enemy, Saul asked his armor-bearer to finish him off. The man was fearful and refused, so Saul took a sword from his armor-bearer and jumped on it. The man, seeing that Saul had died, likewise jumped on his sword and died. That day, Saul, his three sons and all his men died by the sword, as Samuel had predicted. The next day, when the Philistines discovered Saul's body, they cut his head off and took his weapons. But the inhabitants of Jabesh-Gilead gave him a proper burial and fasted seven days.

When David learned that Saul, his sons, and his men had perished, he ripped apart his clothing. Then he turned his anger against the Amalekite who had wounded Saul and was responsible for his death. David mourned Saul, whom he continued to see as God's anointed king, and his son Jonathan, whom he had loved. It is said that he wrote a funeral song in which he referred to Saul and Jonathan as heroes, and ordered it to be taught to all the children of Judah. (1 Sam 29—2 Sam 1)

WHEN LOAMMI RETURNED HOME after his two-year absence, he was a different man. Marine had pictured her lost husband running through the rain in the middle of the night, leaving behind every possession, every material gain that he had accumulated during his itinerant years—running like a man who realized the error of his ways and wanted to push his sins as far away from himself as possible. She had even made a drawing of him kneeling at the feet of Jesus, receiving a new heart and a new mind. But when Loammi came back, it was not what she had expected. Loammi did not make a grand theatrical comeback and a profusive, remorseful confession; he did not beg her to take him back or repent in front of the entire family. He just came back and brought all his belongings. Then, he spoke to her privately, saying:

"I am sorry for everything I've done. I hope that you can forgive me."

That was it. Marine had not considered this possible turn of events, so she was confused as to what to do. She heard her husband talking to a friend over the phone. He was confiding to his friend that he did not deserve to still have a wife and be with his family, and he praised God for the fact that his wife *was* still there. However, Marine did not fully feel that she was there. She did not know if he was repentant; his words did not line up with his actions, and he behaved in ways that he had clearly picked up somewhere else. She saw a different man—a man who had no shame, no vulnerability—a superficial person who acted out the motions of a man but who had no real feelings. She, on the other hand, had *too many* conflicting feelings, and they were hard to control. She thought of screaming at him and throwing him and all his possessions out the door, but instead she froze and did not know how to react. She felt conflicted. The children had grown and adjusted to a life of peace, discovering more autonomy during their dad's absence; they did not welcome his return. But, what would God, the redeemer of the lowly, the savior of the wretched, want?

Marine could not figure out what was going on with Loammi, other than it was not the picture she had painted in her mind or on paper, and she was disappointed. She had prayed so hard for her husband's return, and he had returned, so who was she to tell God that he had not returned the way she wanted him to? Therefore, she decided to give it some time and see.

Loammi had kept the black Cadillac that he had been driving. She hated that car. It was a reminder of his philandering. By God's grace, some months after his return, it was impounded, and since it was not technically his, it was never returned to him. Marine felt that it was as if Loammi was the epitome of Jude 1:23 and had to be pulled away from his sins as a man is pulled from a fire, yet shown mercy mixed with fear, all the while hating his stained garment. He also kept all the music equipment and other gifts that he had accumulated through his affairs—the material gain he had "worked" so hard to obtain—and that reminded Marine that his repentance was only skin deep.

She watched him settle in back home as an onlooker watches a chessboard set before her, not knowing whether she wants to be in or out, and ends up playing the part. Taking her turn, she anticipates her opponent's move by observing the pieces and drawing diagrams in her mind of each possible outcome, all before she decides on her own move. As a child, Marine had played many a chess game with her father; sometimes it would take up to twenty minutes for one of them to decide which move to make. Her dad would start to grab the queen, and at the last second, change his mind and turn to a bishop. Sometimes, you just don't know what to do, so you wait.

One day she did say one thing:

"If you ever cheat on me again, or put your hands on me again, I will leave you and never come back. And I will not care."

Loammi had nodded and walked away, like a dog with his tail between his legs. Even so, they never addressed the conflict. It became the elephant in the room everyone strategically maneuvered around.

Days and weeks passed. Loammi slowly lost his shell and started to open up and speak confidently like the person he once was, but Marine felt that something was missing, that something was gone. Later on, she realized what it was: respect.

"Lord, I am trying to encourage his repentance, but I don't see anything that I can respect about this man! Please give me something to respect about him!"

Somehow Marine believed that the violence would not start up again, because her husband had stooped to the lowest level she could have imagined, and his conscience had to be troubled. He was more guilty than ever. Therefore, without her speaking any words of condemnation, she found comfort in the knowledge that he was bearing his judgement, and deep inside, she wished for him to suffer. It was difficult to change her attitude. She knew that there was bitterness in her heart, and sometimes she would go for a walk to scream and curse his name out loud. Other times, she would find a bit of twisted pleasure in uttering a few words of sarcasm in a very indirect way, as only women know how to do. Condescension became her weapon of choice to avenge the wounds that Loammi had inflicted on her. But of course, that was not very Christian, and she was suffering even when she let her feelings out in this indirect manner.

"I want us to go to counseling," she told him one night.

Loammi reacted as a man typically reacts when his wife asks of him something that matters to her but not to him—that is, with one ear open. He did not take heed nor respond, so Marine insisted:

"If we don't go to counseling, I'm leaving you."

Loammi knew a pastor, and they had their first counseling session a few days later.

Loammi told the man of God everything: every wrong he'd done, how he had hurt his family, that his children did not trust him, that he needed to change and did not know how to. The pastor discerned what was going on with the couple, and his words and wise advice lifted weights that Marine had been carrying on her shoulders for too long, and perhaps Loammi too.

"Pastor," said Loammi, "I'm back home now, and I'm ready to start over. I have repented and apologized to my wife, but I feel like she is bitter and can't let it go. My own daughter now doesn't want me around, and I don't know how we can move on."

"Loammi," concluded the pastor, "you are going to have to prove your loyalty to your family now. You may believe that you are ready to give your family your best, but what they have witnessed is your worst. Your love is now on trial, and you are going to have to take a back seat for a while, until you have proven yourself.

"See," he added, "women and girls, especially, are very gentle, and you cannot impose yourself on them. They remember violence and it takes time to gain their trust again after so much pain has been inflicted. You are going to have to approach them like a man tames a deer."

"Wow, I never saw it that way," replied Loammi.

That day brought a real breakthrough and was healing to their souls. For Marine, it felt as if her husband finally heard everything that she had tried to tell him for years.

They had a few more counseling sessions, but eventually, time went by, and they got busy. Their son moved to college, and by the grace of God, they were able to purchase a home. Loammi had decided to get a degree to pursue a career in business and started attending classes. They decorated their home, and for the most part, there was peace in the house. Everyone had a routine, a job to tend to, and the common pursuit of individual and family happiness.

SOON IT WAS JANUARY again. The below-zero temperatures served as a reminder that those fortunate to have a home out of the cold should be thankful. Those who are fortunate to have the warmth of loved ones at that time of the year should be even more thankful. Those people have too much to lose to take a wrong turn at this time of the year, when it is dark in the mid-afternoon and everyone stays inside for weeks on end.

Loammi had been given another chance and had vowed that things would be different. He believed that he was going to give the best of him to himself and to his family. He had even talked to God about it, and he believed that God had taken away his anger, the root of all sins that consumed him. He had even started to make peace with his children.

Unfortunately, in his euphoria to believe that he was a new man, he had not considered that he may get angry again, so he did not have a plan in place for when that moment came to pass.

It was a Saturday afternoon, the eve of Valentine's day—a time when couples get ready to go out dancing, eat out, and enjoy a moment alone in each other's company, anticipating a declaration and demonstration of their love for one another. Loammi and Marine were home, and Loammi had had a few drinks. For some reason Marine found this to be the perfect time to say something mean and hurtful, to twist the dagger just a little bit by reminding him of his infidelities. Perhaps it was because she was still awaiting a real apology. Perhaps it was because he had not followed up on going to counseling. Perhaps it was because she was tired of seeing him drink again. Perhaps it was because after their daughter had left the house to go to a friend's, he had called them "harlots." And since she was not a two-hundred-pound man, her sword was her mouth:

"The only harlot in this family is you."

Loammi's pride was hit as if by a whip. He lashed out.

"I am sick and tired of your condemnations! I am done being condemned by you; you have nothing good to say!" He stormed out and headed to the bedroom, slamming the door behind him.

THAT EVENING, MARINE HAD invited a friend over for dinner. She was counting on Loammi to calm down, as he had started to play music rather loudly. An awkward dinner, she thought, almost regretting what she had said. But, she made the best of it and ate with her girlfriend. They talked; they enjoyed each other's company. When her friend left, Marine knocked on the bedroom door to make peace with Loammi. He had not calmed down and started to argue again, so she left him alone. She went to the living room and picked up a book she had started reading. It was about setting boundaries with difficult people; things were starting to come into focus about what a relationship should look like. It was time that Marine developed a spine and put into practice some of the strategies that she had read about to not be taken advantage of by unreasonable people. Loammi walked into the kitchen mumbling curse words. He was certainly an unreasonable man. The book explained that while you may love someone, sometimes you have to draw a firm line, be it a strong "no" or a restraining order. So, as Loammi came toward her and started arguing again, Marine suddenly felt justified for all the times she had called the police and all the times she had disapproved of her husband's behavior. The times when she complained about him. The times when she plotted an escape behind his back. The times when she had yelled in his face. When she called him bad names. Loammi's mumbling and growling interrupted her reading. Why could he not ignore her and go away? Why was he still trying to argue? She looked at him, gave him a polite nod, then she looked back at her book. He did not let go.

"What do you have to say, huh? What do you have to say to me, since you're so perfect, since you always have all the right answers?"

"I don't want to talk to you. You're drunk."

"Oh, now all of a sudden you have nothing to say, huh? You're not that smart, are you? You're just a dumb b*&%#."

"F#%@ you!"

Somehow, as soon as she uttered those words, she felt a shudder go down her spine. She had thought those words, but did not fully realize that they had come out of her mouth.

Loammi was furious. "What did you say to me?"

His anger was now kindled. Within seconds, he had grabbed his wife by the neck and started squeezing her tight. Immediately, Marine was transported to an alternate reality. The thought that ran through her head was: I'm going to die. I should have left him when I had a chance. At that moment, she regretted taking him back. She panicked. She prayed to God for help and realized that the survival instinct in a person is strong. She realized that perhaps him cheating was not the worst thing in the world. In fact, at that moment, she thought that she'd rather lose Loammi and live. She begged Loammi to stop, but it seemed that he would not. Please Lord help me, she thought. "I am sorry!" she screamed to her husband, but the words came out as a whisper.

Loammi released his grip. He did let go. Marine went to the bathroom to check her neck injury. He must have punched her as well, for when she looked at the mirror, her face had doubled in size. Her body started to shake. She wanted to call 911, but her right arm was numb, and she could not work her hand to dial the numbers. She was afraid that if she took too long, the intruder in her home would snatch the phone from her.

Loammi looked at her and panicked. "I am a monster," he said. Marine asked him to take her to the hospital, but Loammi debated with himself. What should they say to the doctors? He couldn't go back to jail. An accident, he thought, it would have to be an accident. What would be their story? he asked Marine. It had to sound credible. Meanwhile, all she could think of was that her arm was tingling, her neck hurt, and she was afraid that a new injury would leave lasting damage on her body this time. Moreover, she was afraid to spend any more time trapped with him. She wanted to run far away from him, forever. Loammi waited until morning to rest and sober up so he would not get pulled over by the police. Then, he finally took her to the hospital.

A NORMAL LIFE IS quite a cliché, and most people avoid the term because it often refers to an idealized way of living; yet, finding herself again in a hospital, Marine knew that her life was not normal. She had refused to incriminate her husband—what would be the point?—but she knew this could not go on anymore: this marriage, this union. It was not right. She asked her husband to leave, but he insisted on going home together, and since she was incapacitated and drugged, she could not do much at the moment.

The week that followed was challenging. They were living a lie: for him, it was the lie that they just needed to love each other better and she would get over it, and for her, it was a lie of omission—she was plotting an escape somehow, as soon as she was physically able again. Then there were the lies that were told to their children, who thought Mommy had had an accident. For Marine, the most difficult moments came each night her husband was still under her roof. Her heart started pounding every time Loammi turned off the bedroom light and his shadow stood at the door. Though the odds of him assaulting her again were low, the images of that awful night played over and over in her head.

Now was the time when he wanted to talk about God again, read the Bible, and talk about love. Loammi played the radio, tuned to a Christian station, almost non-stop. He turned the volume up when he heard a sermon that discussed marital relationships, as if to convince Marine that their marriage was God's best plan for them. But in the years that Marine had had to live without her husband, God had uprooted some of the biblical misunderstandings that Loammi had taught her, the first one being that oneness in marriage, like oneness with Jesus, does not absolve either partner of their personal choices and responsibilities. In other words, God does not want puppet wives who worship their husbands, and that is what she had become by devoting all her time, care, and heart to praying for Loammi's redemption. Marine could see that her husband had not changed his destructive ways in all these years. In fact, things had gotten worse, and all her prayers and cries had failed. Perhaps it was time to find out why God was not healing this marriage and what his will was.

The radio was playing a podcast, and a sentence caught her attention: "You can't tell a narcissist that he is wrong." Marine listened and found some pieces of information that made her think. Perhaps Loammi was a narcissist, or perhaps she herself had gone too far trying to be her husband's savior, and in seeking to honor him, she had failed to adequately love herself and her children. According to her research, a characteristic of empaths is that they put others's needs above their own. While the Word of God does say that a Christian should esteem others above himself or herself, it also says to rebuke those who sin and not be influenced by them, but to influence them instead. In her attempt to love her husband, Marine had become an enabler of his sins and had failed to put God first. It was now clear to her that this marriage had become a prison that she had helped build by allowing Loammi to think for her. How ironic, for someone who considered herself an intellectual to feel so dumb. And now, she could no longer rationalize the current state of their marriage. It was not teamwork; it was not a friendship. It had lost its roots. Though she had love for her husband, despite his tormented spirit, she now saw him as unstable and dangerous. And most importantly, he was not willing to change. She was housebound by her injuries, and she feared him all over again.

It was Friday afternoon. Loammi left the house to run an errand. Marine begged God to take him away and not allow him to come back home. Let him be pulled over, or have a small accident, even, she cried within. But a few hours later, he returned.

"Guess who I ran into today?" he announced. "An old friend from high school! . . . What's wrong with you; why are you squirming like that? You're in pain? Well, it must be psychological, because the doctor said you're just fine."

The next day, Saturday afternoon, Loammi left again to run another errand. Marine kneeled and prayed again to God: "Lord, I beg of you, I cannot take this anymore, I cannot stay with him, please remove him from my life, please do something about it, please!"

And then, she heard the voice of God as a gentle and solid thought emanating from the back of her mind:

"No. I want *you* to do something about it."

The next day, Marine told one of her friends what happened. The day after, Monday morning, her friend took her to the courthouse to file a restraining order. The police removed her husband from their home, along with some of his belongings and a check he had just cashed. Marine let him take the car because it was very cold outside, and she wanted him to be able to make it on his own.

FOR TWO YEARS, THEY lived apart. Marine found it more difficult than she would have expected to watch her husband decline again by following one bad choice after another. One day in the winter, she agreed to meet him by her place of work during her lunch break. When he pulled up with their old Ford, she realized that she had forgotten how raggedy her car really was. As he rolled the window down, she was surprised to see him unshaven and lean. He had lost weight—and power. How come he did not manage to find another Cadillac girl? she wondered. But as she talked with him, she could tell that the person before her eyes was a struggling man who did not care to play any more games, and she had compassion on him.

"Baby," he said, "I am not asking you to spend time with me or even talk to me. I am not asking that of our daughter, even. If this is what you want, I will respect it. But I am trying to stay in school and do better things. Give myself better chances. I don't have anywhere to go. Is it possible for me to go home during the day while you guys are at work and school, so I have a quiet and safe place to study?"

Once again, Marine felt sorry for him. He was as a lost child who, unlike her, had not mastered the art of doing homework in the eye of the storm, like with parents yelling nearby or a drunk husband playing loud music.

"You can take this key to our home; it is the bottom lock. I will leave the top lock open. You will need to respect the time frame we agree on and be gone by the time we come back. If you don't, even once, you will lose this privilege, and I will change the lock."

Loammi agreed, and for a time, he respected the agreement. He never stayed beyond his time, and his texts revealed gratefulness at first, then frustration and resentment. Every time she got home after he had been in the apartment, Marine wondered if Loammi had truly been studying. His boxed belongings were opened, and though he made an effort to pick up after himself, she knew he had spent his time looking for her personal items. One day, while he was at her house, she received an angry text.

Why did you get rid of the washer and dryer set?

You know it was broken, she replied, *and you told me yourself it was a fire hazard. I was able to clean the original washing machine, and it works. I got rid of the old one.*

You shouldn't have done that! he wrote back. *It is my washer and dryer!*

What do you mean, it is yours? You never do laundry.

It is mine. My machine, my house, my home! You guys should be the ones to be kicked out in the cold, and I should be in my home with my dog!

Saddened and a bit troubled, Marine responded carefully.

Have you gotten some work done? I hope you are keeping up with school. Let me know when you're gone. I will be back at six.

You think you rule the world? How can you give me orders like I'm your slave? You think you can tell me what to do? You can't tell me what to do. You'll see.

We have an agreement, she composed politely, but firmly. *If you break it, I will call the police.*

F#%@ the police, and f#%@ you! I'm bound by no man but God, and God will make you pay for all the evil you do. You think you're so sleek, but you will see, my God will judge you, you monster, and it will be too late then!

Marine texted her daughter to not go home that evening. When she arrived at her apartment, Loammi was gone, but he had made sure to make his voice heard. A long streak was imprinted on the laminate flooring, from the hallway almost all the way to the bedroom. How did this happen? Broken glass. From a picture frame in the bedroom. The picture was missing but Marine recognized the frame. It was her favorite wedding photo because Loammi looked so happy in it. Gentle and full of innocent joy, like the real him.

In her heart, Marine still heard his soul scream for help; the texts revealed that his state of mind was still unstable. She had a hard time giving up on the man she saw he could become, but she understood that God was undoing this relationship because it was not good.

For a while, she did agree to go to counseling sessions with Loammi and the pastor whom he had involved in their dirty laundry before, until the man of God concluded that they should get serious abusive relationship advice. Loammi registered in an abuse program, and Marine saw a female therapist recommended by the pastor.

Seeing a therapist allowed Marine to think objectively for the first time in years. Because she was a Christian, Dr. J. understood the driving force behind Marine's actions. She did not try to diagnose what was wrong with Loammi as Marine had first hoped. Instead, she focused on helping Marine understand how she had lived her life and how God saw her.

"Why did I put up with all this?" asked Marine.

Dr. J. smiled. She had a gentle but confident voice, a humble beauty, and an answer for everything.

"You've been used to this feeling of walking on eggshells because it was familiar to you when you were a child," explained the therapist. "But now you are an adult, and no one has the right to make you feel like a child."

Marine concluded: "I guess I've married my dad."

"I've been saying that from the beginning," said Dr. J.

Marine asked: "Am I a co-dependent empath?"

Her interlocutor laughed. "I think you've developed this pattern, but you are trying to get out of it."

Her voice was soft. She listened first, and then she spoke. Her words were soothing, without judgement.

"You have to make your own decision. I am not telling you what to do, but you need to pay attention to the pattern that exists between you and your husband, and be realistic in your expectations."

She pointed Marine to the Song of Solomon, and Marine read in the Word of God what love is supposed to look like: like Jesus, the shepherd is a protector (". . . his banner over me was love" [2:4]). In the shepherd's eyes, the Shulamite is the most beautiful woman of all and he does not cease to be taken by her beauty; he is good to her ("As the lily among the thorns, so is my love among the daughters" [2:20]). The shepherd's fascination with and love for his bride makes her flourish so that everything she touches bears fruit ("Thy teeth are like a flock of sheep that are even shorn, which came up from the washing; whereof everyone bears twins, and none is barren among them" [4:2]). He still enjoys her when she gains or loses a few pounds, or when her skin loses the elasticity of its youth ("I said, I will go up to the palm tree, I will take hold of the boughs thereof: now also thy breasts shall be as clusters of the vine, and the smell of thy nose like apples" [7:8]). Because his love is anchored in the redemption of Christ, he finds no fault in her ("Thou art fair, my love; there is no fault in thee" [4:7]). Once she has given herself to him, the Shulamite is able to trust her lover's faithfulness ("I am my beloved's, and his desire is toward me" [7:10]).

Meanwhile, Loammi continued to exhibit the same pattern of sudden effusive professions of love and hate. He did not pick himself up and continued to have an unstable living situation. After two years of not seeing results, and feeling guided by the Holy Spirit, Marine knew that God was leading her to divorce her husband. She felt the Lord had slowly and gently pulled her away from a very unhealthy attachment, and she understood that in some ways, Loammi's constant needs, demands, and attention-seeking behaviors had taken the place of God in her life, much like an idol, and it was time that Marine let him go.

From the moment she filed the divorce papers until the final judgment, Marine felt led and supported by the Holy Spirit. She was sad for the love they once had, for the loss of the hope that they could be happy, but she knew God had to cut off their bad and destructive marriage, which did not honor him. He was with her all the way, and as time went by, she felt healthier, stronger, even happier. She learned to relax again and stopped smoking. She learned to enjoy the smiles of a neighbor and the caress of the sun. Most importantly, her home became peaceful, and the family felt free to move around without fear, without drama, without abuse. Marine had to learn to let go, and it helped to see her children now acting more alive than ever. Watching them move fearlessly into their future was a reminder that she had made the right decision, and her story—though not the one she had hoped for—was under God's control.

Conclusion

"For the LORD God of Israel says That He hates divorce, For it covers one's garment with violence," Says the LORD of hosts. "Therefore take heed to your spirit, That you do not deal treacherously."

—MAL 2:16 (NKJV)

Thoughts from the Author

There is only so much someone you love and are committed to can do to you until you cannot take it anymore. A marriage takes the commitment of two people, and we reap what we sow. As God himself divorced Israel for its abominations and repeated betrayals, he warns us of the natural consequences to earthly and spiritual affairs. If love is sown in a marriage, then it thrives. If there is understanding, communication, patience, and respect, it survives. But if a man or woman abuses the love that he or she is given, and spits on the precious gift of God that is a marriage, God himself will not defend it. Why let two people continually hurt one another? How does such a marriage honor God?

When I divorced my husband, I felt like I was giving up the battle for his soul, and that I had failed my mission. But when I read Malachi again, it dawned on me that when God says that he hates divorce, he explains that divorce is the natural consequence of continual mistreatment, abuse, betrayal, and destruction that a spouse inflicts on his or her partner—his or her companion—and that is what he hates. God also hates a proud look, a lying tongue, violence, wickedness, feet that are quick to do evil, a false witness, and one who sows discord. Those evil and carnal dispositions are often dominant in a failed marriage, causing its breakdown. If marriage is supposed to reflect the beauty of Christ and his bride, the church, why would God keep together a marriage that shames his name? God does away with what is wrong or bad, and that is why it says in the Bible that "it repented the Lord that he had made man on the earth" (Gen 6:6). I have sometimes wondered if God ever regretted bringing me and my husband together.

This is not a book about winning; it is a book about learning to lose. I have no doubt that God guided me to divorce my husband. I can see now how withered I would have become—assuming I would still be alive—if I had not made that decision. But it is a loss, nonetheless. For me it is the loss of a beautiful dream of transformation, and for my ex-husband the loss of the best gift he's been given in his life: the opportunity to have a loving and stable family. And it is sad no matter how you look at it.

This life is short, and no matter what cards we are dealt, we have to work with them and use them to our best advantage, especially when they are not the cards we wanted. Whether you are dealing with addiction, anger, mental illness, or a physical disability, it is your cross to bear and to overcome. If God did not take away the thorn in the flesh of Paul of Tarsus, he must expect us to deal with our own problems. To do something about it and not use excuses. Jesus said that each man ought to pick up his cross and follow him. He makes things possible; he makes things better and life worthwhile, yet we still go through what he has allowed to come our way as a result of our sinful world. Our trials are inevitable.

Marriage is meant to be a beautiful relationship. It is the most intimate and the strongest bond we can develop with a person who is not inherently lovable, like our children. Marriage is beautiful and difficult, and love fulfills and contains risks, because it makes you vulnerable to loss. And in my story, we all lost.

While my children are healthier without a toxic father breathing down their necks and without having to worry about my safety every day, I still believe nothing would have been better than if they had witnessed the real transformation of a broken man into a man made whole by Jesus. They still have to pick up the pieces of how their parents' dysfunctional relationship affected their childhood, and only God knows how this will affect them as they find a partner and start a family of their own.

Even though I now live a good life free from abuse, filled with love, works, and rewards, and even though I entertain the hope that God could bring a new and better husband into my life, I still believe that it would have been a glorious thing for my destructive husband to have done a complete 180 and surrendered to God. Those stories happen; it is just not my story.

Seeing my story unravel through the adventures of David and King Saul has taught me a lot about why God allowed my marriage to die. I have learned that love is tough. Love is not bending over backwards and accepting anything—it is knowing when to say "yes" and when to say "no," which was hard for me to do. Love is putting nothing and no one above God himself; it is being willing to surrender anything to God's will, even if it does not look like what we envision and dream of. Love is being willing to lose, for in the end, God has the last word.

MAY YOU FIND YOUR story, learn from it, and live it without regret. There are plenty of other stories in the Bible. Hosea's adulterous wife Gomer was made whole, and they did live happily ever after. On the other hand, Nabal, Abigail's husband, was killed by God for his wickedness. There are many stories in the Bible to learn from; may God reveal the one that speaks to you, and let it be a blessing to teach you about your life. May you find your story and understand that God loves you. Because all biblical narrations tell us about God's love for humanity and that his desires for us are good. And ultimately, the most important marriage is the one we will share with Christ.

This life on earth is a passage through time. Sometimes you have to love someone from afar and turn him or her over to God. I will always have love for my ex-husband; he will always be family in some sense, and even today, after the pain, the abuse, the hurt, and the loss, I still believe that God will use even this divorce to reach him. Everything God touches bears fruit, and he uses it all: the joys and the pains, the blessings and the tragedies, the gains and the losses, the failures and the successes. I wish for you to find him as the light of your own journey!

Discussion and Self-Reflection Topics

Psychologists explain that while we all possess to some degree the qualities that are present in unhealthy individuals, and we are all guilty of contributing to malfunctions in our own lives and possibly those of others, the difference between healthy and *clinically* unhealthy individuals is that healthy individuals are able to function in most areas of their lives, while unhealthy individuals are not. Typically, unhealthy individuals demonstrate a consistent inability to maintain stability in various aspects of their personal lives, be it their relationships, or their employment. According to Bill Eddy, problems arise from extreme behaviors. "Each of these people has an extreme version of what we call *high-conflict personality*. Unlike most of us, who normally try to resolve or diffuse conflicts, people with high-conflict personalities (HCPs) respond to conflicts by compulsively *increasing* them."[1]

---

1. Eddy, Bill. *5 Types of People Who Can Ruin Your Life*, 6

Lundy Bancroft has paved the way for understanding the cycle of abuse by studying the behavior of abusive men and counseling them and their families for decades. His book *Why Does He Do That? Inside the Minds of Angry and Controlling Men* is among the most cited sources of information in abuse programs; in it, the renowned therapist concludes that men who abuse their loved ones do so not because they may have a mental illness, but perhaps in spite of that possibility. In other words, according to Bancroft, men who are abusive make the choice to be so, consciously or not.[2]

In this memoir, the stories of King Saul and David and of Loammi and Marine emphasize several character traits which may be shared by various types of abusive individuals: charisma ("The Charmer"), rebellion ("The Rebel"), depression ("The Depressed Personality"), narcissism ("The Narcissist"), jealousy ("The Jealous Type"), anger ("The Angry Man"), unreliability ("The Promise-Breaker"), self-victimization ("The Victim"), apology-making ("The Apologizer"), unfaithfulness ("The Adulterer"), and deception ("The Con Artist"). The questions below can be used to guide further reflection or discussions.

1. In your own life, have you experienced any or several of those traits being dominant in a person you have had a relationship with, or in the relationship of others? Explain. Keep in mind that there may be more characteristics besides those described in this memoir.

2. Have these characteristics caused significant dysfunction or perhaps destruction in the person who exhibited these traits, or for their family members or loved ones, including yourself? Explain.

3. Are you able to describe which traits in particular pose problems, when exaggerated? Write them down or name them and explain.

4. How have you dealt with these difficult situations, or how do you think you would respond if you had to deal with someone with some of these characteristics? Think of one character trait at a time.

5. After reading this memoir, has your perception of abusive men (or women) and abused women (or men) changed? Explain.

6. While characters, like people, should not be reduced to their racial representations, if Marine had been a woman of color, how do you think this would have changed her access to resources and ability to receive help? Explain.

7. In what ways does racial injustice add complexity to issues of abuse and domestic violence? Can you explain?

2. Bancroft, Lundy. *Why Does He Do That?*, 319

8. If you are in a difficult relationship, or want to help someone else who is, what tools could you use to do that?

9. What passages in the Bible cover the topic of abuse? Explain or discuss the situation, the biblical perspective provided, as well as your personal take from it.

10. What other books have you read or shows have you watched on the topic of abuse, and what good counsel have you gotten from them?

Bibliography

Bancroft, Lundy. *Why Does He Do That? Inside the Minds of Angry and Controlling Men.* New York: Berkley Nooks, 2002.

Bottke, Allison. *Setting Boundaries with Difficult People: Six Steps to Sanity for Challenging Relationships.* Oregon: Harvest House, 2011.

Eddy, Bill. *5 Types of People Who Can Ruin Your Life: Identifying and Dealing with Narcissists, Sociopaths, and Other High-Conflict Personalities.* Oregon: Tarcher Perigee, 2018.

Made in the USA
Monee, IL
27 April 2024

57594867R00081